❈ BELOVED LAND

An Oral History of Mexican Americans in Southern Arizona

Collected and Edited by Patricia Preciado Martin 🏷 With Photographs by José Galvez

The University of Arizona Press ◀ Tucson

The University of Arizona Press
© 2004 The Arizona Board of Regents
First Printing

∞ This book is printed on acid-free, archival-quality paper.
Manufactured in the United States of America

09   08   07   06   05   04   6   5   4   3   2   1

Library of Congress Cataloging-in-Publication Data

Beloved land : an oral history of Mexican Americans in southern Arizona /
collected and edited by Patricia Preciado Martin ; with photographs by
José Galvez.
         p. cm.
   ISBN 0-8165-2382-7 (paper: alk. paper)
   ISBN 0-8165-2409-2 (cloth: alk. paper)
   1. Mexican Americans–Arizona–Biography. 2. Mexican Americans–Arizona–
Pictorial works. 3. Ranchers–Arizona–Biography. 4. Ranchers–Arizona–Pictorial
works. 5. Mexican American families–Arizona–Social life and customs. 6. Mexican
American families–Arizona–History. 7. Ranch life–Arizona–History. 8. Arizona–
Social life and customs. 9. Arizona–Social life and customs–Pictorial works.
10. Oral history. I. Martin, Patricia Preciado. II. Galvez, José, 1949–
   F820.M5B35 2004
   979.1'70046872'00922–dc22

                                                                    2003015503

British Library Cataloguing-in-Publication Data
A catalogue record for this book is available from the British Library.

Publication of this book is made possible in part by the proceeds of a permanent
endowment created with the assistance of a Challenge Grant from the National
Endowment for the Humanities, a federal agency.

Every day that is born into the world comes like a burst of music and rings itself all the day through; and thou shalt make it a dance, a dirge, or a life march, as thou wilt.

—*St. Frances de Sales*

To our wonderful children, Elena and Jim. Because you have danced the joyful dance on this beloved land.

Contents

Photographs

Foreword *Thomas E. Sheridan*

Patricia Preciado Martin crafts her oral histories with the soul of a poet. When you turn the pages of this book, you will learn many particulars about Mexican ranch life in southern Arizona during the twentieth century, but you will not find historical particulars. Instead, this book is about the soul of a people whose roots run as deep as the mesquite trees that have warmed and sheltered them in the land they call home.

The roots of their world of family ranchos are nearly five hundred years old. It is a world forged in the great deserts of North America, where Spaniards and their mestizo descendants pushed northward and left Mesoamerica behind, a world that could be entered only on horseback, for horses made the world possible. The world of Mexican ranchos is flickering and dying in southern Arizona, but it lives on in Sonora, Chihuahua, Coahuila, Nuevo León, Tamaulipas, Durango, and Baja California. When I read the stories of the men and women interviewed here, they transport me back to Cucurpe, Sonora, where I lived for a year in the early 1980s. My friends in Cucurpe venerate the same santos, prepare the same foods, and make their living in the same ways as the people in this book.

These men and women are not the ranchers of Hollywood stereotype. None of them owned big spreads. Many of them worked other jobs—as miners, railroad workers, housekeepers, construction workers—to pay their bills. But running cattle and tilling the dry Arizona soil gave them their identities and connected them to their pasts. Life on the ranchos embraced them, enriched them, tested them. During the depression, it gave them food when other people went hungry. During the postwar migration to the cities—*del rancho al barrio*—it gave them refuge and a sense of themselves as people of the soil.

When we think of Spaniards in Mexico, we often conjure images of conquistadores searching for gold or silver. But many immigrants from the Iberian Peninsula were peasants who came from villages where people cultivated small plots of land and raised small herds of livestock on village common lands. When these resourceful individuals sailed across the Atlantic, they brought their agropastoralist way of life with them. Stock raising and farming were not mutually exclusive occupations, but rather symbiotic strategies that nearly every household pursued. Together they provided most of the food a household required to sustain itself on an isolated and often dangerous frontier.

As geographer Terry Jordan points out in his magisterial *Cattle Frontiers of North America* (1993), the Hispanic pioneers who moved up the Mesa Central into Nueva Vizcaya (modern-day Durango and Chihuahua) and on into New Mexico raised far more sheep than cattle. But those who advanced north along the Pacific Coast ran more cattle than sheep. They were heirs of a free-range cattle industry that developed in the salt marshes of the Guadalquivir River in Andalusia, not on the windswept plains of Castile or Extremadura. Their *corriente* cattle, long-legged and long-horned, adapted well to the thorn forests of Sinaloa, the deserts of Sonora, and the mountains of the Sierra Madre Occidental. They could fight off mountain lions or wolves and walk miles a day to water. These tough, cantankerous animals enabled Mexican rancheros to convert nonedible grasses and shrubs into beef, milk, cheese, rawhide, tallow, soap, and other products mentioned in these pages.

Corrientes could be worked only on horseback. There were no fences on the northern frontier. People depended on horses for just about everything—to round up cattle, to get back and forth between ranches and towns, to flee from or take revenge against their enemies. Both girls and boys learned horsemanship at an early age. The alchemy of horse and rider transmuted reliance on horses into an abiding love of horses. Nearly all major celebrations and religious fiestas featured horse races. Luis Gastellum's father, Santiago, competed as a professional team roper for fifty years. When I drank with men in Cucurpe, they talked about horses, not women. "When he was eighty years old, my father gave a roping exhibition at a ranch just east of Nogales on the Patagonia Road," Luis Gastellum recalled. "It is said that his ease and grace on a horse, even at that advanced age, were something to see!"

For these reasons, ranching and cowboying exercised a hold on the imaginations of the people in this book, especially the men, far out of proportion to the dollars or pesos it put in their pocketbooks. Ramón de la Ossa expressed it best when he told Patricia:

> Now that I'm back in Tucson, I go out to the ranch as often as I can. As soon as I retire, I'm going to go back there and live full-time. Before I moved back full-time to help my dad, ranching started getting in my blood. I started feeling that way shortly after my mother passed away. I would visit my dad, and even though he was getting older—he was seventy-six years old when Mother passed away—he was still pretty strong. He still rode horseback; he still roped and did all the ranch chores.
>
>   Anyway, it got in my blood, and I couldn't get rid of it. I got the feeling, "I want to do this!" It got so deep in my veins that I can almost taste it. I'll be on a horse riding the range, riding the fence line—all the duties of a rancher out in the open. It's an overwhelming feeling that I get in my mind and body. There's no turning back.

Many of the men and women in this book could also taste the soil they turned over with their plows. They had an enduring hunger for the earth—a benevolent addiction even when most income to support their families came from their day jobs on the railroads or in the mines. Elena Vásquez Cruz, who was born on the Sosa Ranch along the San Pedro River, remembers her father's rancho at Redington: "My father wanted to plant everything under the sun, and he did. He raised alfalfa, corn, wheat, barley, lentils, peanuts, peas, yams, and garbanzos. He planted tobacco." Agatha Cota Gastellum, who was born in Tumacacori, recalled the family homestead along the Santa Cruz River: "My father was a farmer. He had a little orchard around the house and grew grapes, peaches, apricots, quince, pomegranates, and other kinds of fruit that he experimented with. On his 160 acres he planted corn, beans, potatoes, tomatoes, garbanzos, fava beans, teparies, chile peppers, and watermelons."

These lists of crops reveal another fundamental reality of Mexican ranch life—the vibrant fusion of the so-called Old World of Eurasia and the New World of the Americas triggered by what biological historians call the "Columbian Exchange." Corn, beans, squash, chilies, teparies, potatoes, tomatoes, and tobacco were all plants that had been domesticated in the Americas. Wheat, barley, alfalfa, lentils, fava beans, and most fruits and vegetables, on the other hand, came from Eurasia or Africa, as did cattle, horses, pigs, goats, and sheep. Most of the Old World cultigens were frost tolerant; most of the New World crops were not. The transoceanic exchange of seeds and nursery stock enabled Mexican farmers in southern Arizona to cultivate their fields year round. If you drive down the river valleys of central or eastern Sonora, you can see the Columbian Exchange at work in the patchwork of fields along the floodplain–Old World green in the winter, New World green in the summer. The humble but mouthwatering foods described in this book represent a truly international cuisine.

This book pulses with life–food, family, music, work. But it is also an elegy. A few of these families have held onto their ranchos, but most have lost their land to Anglo ranchers or Anglo developers. This hard, self-reliant way of life is nearly gone north of the international border. But then, family agriculture in the United States is fighting a losing battle against agribusiness, subdivisions, and the globalization of food production.

The end of this way of life is a profound loss. Rural communities are unraveling even as cities fling their bedroom and recreational offspring beyond metropolitan borders. Our landscapes are being depersonalized, leached of land-based cultures and their intimate knowledge of place. Twenty years ago, Patricia and I worked together on the Mexican Heritage Project at the Arizona Historical Society, a grassroots effort Patricia helped found. Tired of having their history ignored by Arizona institutions of culture, Patricia, Belén Ramírez, Joe Noriega, and others volunteered countless hours to reclaim that history by collecting family photographs and recording oral histories. I provided the academic trappings, directing students who ransacked Spanish-language newspapers, census manuscripts, city directories, and other archival sources to complement personal accounts of family life. Patricia and I formed a life-long friendship then–one based on a fierce love of the rancho life she has so lovingly recorded in these interviews. Patricia wrote the foreword to *Los Tucsonenses*, my first book, published in 1986. It is one of the honors of my life to return the favor. The life described in these pages deserves to be remembered. It was far richer than life in the southern Arizona countryside is now.

Works Cited

Jordan, Terry G. *North American Cattle-Ranching Frontiers: Origins, Diffusion, and Differentiation.* Albuquerque: University of New Mexico Press, 1993.

Sheridan, Thomas E. *Los Tucsonenses: The Mexican Community in Tucson, 1854–1941.* Tucson: University of Arizona Press, 1986.

Acknowledgments

I offer a very special *gracias con todo corazón* to all the individuals in this book who opened their homes and their hearts to me and entrusted me with their life stories. *Estoy agradecida también* to their families, who often graciously contributed information during the interviews, lent family photographs to me, and reviewed the transcripts. I only hope to honor them and the future generations with this treasure of memories. I am especially indebted to my husband, Jim, who provides sustenance and love as I "follow my bliss" of documenting the history and heritage of Mexican American people.

Gracias, also, to those individuals who introduced me to their families: Irma S. Moreno, for introducing me to Carlotta Parra Rodríguez Sotomayor; Carlotta's daughter, Carmen, and son, Ernie, for sharing their family anecdotes; Gilbert Mungaray, for telling me about his mother, Elena Vásquez Cruz; Peter Mendivil, for telling me about the Mendivil Brothers' Ranch, and Fernando Mendivil, for helping me to get in touch with Teresa Gradillas and Tim Mendivil; Diana Hadley, for helping me to locate Ramón de la Ossa; Steve Gastellum for introducing me to his parents, Agatha Cota Gastellum and Luis Acuña Gastellum; and Chayo Franco, for telling me about his aunt, the centenarian Ramona Benítez Franco. A special thank you to Josefina Mungaray, who gave me permission to include her beautiful poem "Añoranzas del Vaquero Rafael Cruz" in Rafael's chapter, and to Jay Dusard, photographer extraordinaire, who generously gave me permission to reprint his beautiful photograph of Rosamel and Ramón de la Ossa in Ramón's chapter. Without these individuals' help, this book would not have been possible.

Thanks also to University of Arizona Press acquiring editor Patti Hartmann and director Chris Szuter for believing in this book; to in-house editor Nancy Arora for her willingness to answer all my trivial questions; and to Annie Barva, copy editor, for enlightened editing. Last but not least, *gracias a* Dr. Thomas Sheridan—scholar, author, *estimado amigo*—for honoring this book with a foreword and for his *cariño para nuestra raza*.

Introduction

Cuatro milpas tan solo han quedado
Del ranchito que era mío
¡Ay, ay, ay, ay!
De aquella casita, tan blanca y bonita
Todo terminó.

Si me prestas tus ojos morena
Los llevo en el alma que miren allá
Los despojos de aquella casita
Tan blanca y bonita lo triste que está.
(Refrán)

Los potreros están sin ganado
Todito se ha acabado
¡Ay, ay, ay, ay!
Ya no hay palomas
Ni hiedras ni aromas
Todo terminó.

Cuatro milpas que tanto quería
Pues mi madre las cuidaba,
¡Ay, ay, ay, ay!
Si verás que solas
Ya no hay amapolas
Ni hierbas de olor.*

*"Las Cuatro Milpas" by Jose F. Elizondo and Belisario Garcia De Jesús. Copyright © 1961 by Promotora Hispano Americana De Musica, S.A. All rights administered by Peer International Corporation. Copyright © renewed. International rights secured. Used by permission. All rights reserved.

Four fields are all that remain
Of that little ranch of mine
Ay, ay, ay, ay!
And nothing is left
Of my pretty white house.

If you lend me your eyes my dark one
I'll carry them in my soul so they can see
How sad are the remains
Of my pretty white house.
(Refrain)

The ranch is without cattle
Everything is finished
Ay, ay, ay, ay!
There are no doves
Or fragrant vines
All is finished.

Those four fields that I loved so
For my mother cared for them!
Ay, ay, ay, ay!
If you could only see how lonely they are
There are no more flowers
Or sweet-smelling herbs.

   A few years ago, Teresa Mendivil Gradillas, whose parents as well as maternal and paternal ancestors had ranched and farmed in the area of Benson, Arizona, and in the fertile valley of the San Pedro River north of Benson, visited the
historical colonial village of Mesilla, New Mexico, which is now a popular tourist attraction. "I went out to sit in the plaza," she recounted, "while my daughter
was shopping in one of the stores. There was a man and a woman in the plaza
who were playing the guitar and singing the old Mexican song about ranches
called 'Cuatro Milpas,' and I started to cry. When my grandson saw me, he got

worried and went back to get my daughter. 'What's wrong, Mother?' my daughter asked. 'Don't you feel well?' 'It's nothing, *hija*,' I told her. 'It's just when I hear the song "Cuatro Milpas," it reminds me of our family ranch, and it makes me sentimental.'"

The story of the Mendivil family is a story told and retold by legions of Mexican American families in the Southwest whose roots and history are tied to *la tierra*, the land. It is difficult now to imagine and appreciate fully the cultural, spiritual, and linguistic legacy of and the economic and intellectual contributions made by the pioneer Hispano and Mexicano families in "El Norte." So much of the material evidence of the land grants, homesteads, and other ranching and farming settlements has almost completely disappeared in the encroaching development and growth of the Sunbelt cities of the twentieth and twenty-first centuries.

Even though chambers of commerce and tourist bureaus promote and even reconstruct the romantic image of the cowboy and rancher in the Southwest for visitors, retirees, and transplants from the Midwest and the East, little of the true historical nature of the ranchero and vaquero legacy is attributed to settlers of Mexican descent. At best they replicate "old towns" with staged shoot-outs, cantina girls, and gift shops selling plaster garden statues of sleeping Mexicans to gullible tourists. Rarely are there any accurate and respectful depictions of the hard-working and persevering Hispanic pioneers who settled in the greater Southwest, in some instances before it was even part of the United States. Yet so much of what we value in our own contemporary lifestyle is based on the values and culture of the original cowboys, ranchers, and farmers who sacrificed and labored so much when they settled this land.

Where there are now freeway interchanges, suburban housing tracts, gated communities, shopping centers, and golf courses, there were at one time vital, innovative, and close-knit communities of Hispano settlers who brought with them the skills of living off the land that were rooted both in the European culture of Spain and in the mestizo and indigenous cultures of Mexico. The melting adobes of their beloved ranchos, which they built with the aid of family and friends, can occasionally be glimpsed alongside a highway. Facing the bulldozer on the edge of a new retirement or gated community is a gnarled fruit tree or a fence of nopales struggling to survive the absence of a nurturing hand. Hidden among the canyons and hills and plains are the tilting crosses of the family cemeteries, which survive as forgotten tributes to a people whose voices have been silenced not just by death, but by the benign neglect of scholars and historians. As we gaze out over the landscape of our past, this is the heritage we must recapture and embrace for the enlightenment of generations to come.

This is not a book about the powerful or the wealthy, the famous or the political. It is a book that documents, in the voices of ten pioneers, the history that thousands of us of Mexican descent share through our ancestors who came to Arizona and lived off the land. It offers the stories of hardy individuals who settled with their families in the often isolated and far-flung regions of Arizona. Their stories are our stories. They were courageous, self-reliant, and self-taught. They had faith not only in their God, but in themselves, their families, and their communities. These stories are about successes and failures, joys and sorrows, love and loss, beginnings and endings, labors and celebrations, solemn religious vigils with prayers and fiestas with music and dance. They are about interdependence as well as independence, about struggles as well as harmony with the land, but mostly about love affairs with the land and a way of life that is rapidly disappearing.

Don Manuel Ramírez's destiny propelled him from a prosperous hacienda in Aguascalientes, Mexico, to a vegetable farm in Texas and then to the cotton fields in Marana, Arizona, where he worked as a migrant laborer along with his wife and children. He later settled his family on a few acres of land west of the Santa Cruz River. "He worked repairing freight cars for the Pacific Fruit Express Railroad," his son John recounted. "After a full day of work he would return home and hitch his horse up to the plow and work in his beloved milpa until it grew dark. And he never planted seedlings. He would save the best seed from one year to the next and use them for the crops he planted—vegetables, flowers, and herbs." "No one grew corn sweeter than my father," recalled his daughter, Angie Ramírez Valenzuela. "In his later years, when he was infirm and we had to move him to an apartment that had no yard, he kept a can of dirt under the sink so that he could run his fingers through the soil that had nourished him and his family for so many years. He told us that he did that so he would never forget where he came from."

This collection of oral histories is offered as a gift from our elders. It is a legacy of pride that will empower us so that we, like Don Manuel Ramírez, will remember our roots and our ties to la tierra. Ours is an enduring culture. Our ranch homes and fields, our chapels and corrals may have been bulldozed by progress or renovated into spas and guest ranches that never whisper our ancestors' names or retrace their footsteps with respect and gratitude. The story of our beautiful and resilient heritage will never be silenced, however, as long as we remember to run our fingers through the nourishing and nurturing soil of our history and sing the names and the stories of our *antepasados,* ancestors, to the generations to come as if they were a litany.

As poet Josefina Mungaray put it when writing of her father-in-law, the renowned vaquero Rafael Cruz, "The echo of [his] voice / Is still strong and alive."

Beloved Land

Carlotta Parra Rodríguez
Sotomayor looks out over the
land that, beginning in the
1880s, was her husband's
family's ranch in northwest
Tucson. Behind her on the
right is the ranch house in
which her husband, Roberto,
and later their ten children
were raised. Photo by José
Galvez (2000).

Carlotta Parra Rodríguez Sotomayor

I was born in Tucson on November 3, 1913, at the ranch homesteaded by my parents near River Road and Campbell Avenue. My father's name was Francisco Valencia Rodríguez, and my mother's name was María Antonia Parra. I was the eighth of thirteen children. My mother had a Mormon midwife. My father was born in 1872 and came to Tucson with his mother and grandmother and two sisters from Hermosillo, Sonora, Mexico, when he was about six years old. My father's mother, Marcela, eventually married Aniceto Rodríguez, and my father took that surname. My father's mother and his stepfather had a ranch that they homesteaded on River Road and Stone Avenue, where the Starbucks Coffee Shop and On the Border Restaurant are now.

My mother, María Antonia Parra, was born in 1883 in Vulture, Arizona, a mining town close to Wickenburg. My maternal grandparents' names were Carlos Clemente Villaseñor Cabello Parra and Telésfora Pérez Velasco Parra. My grandfather Clemente was educated in a monastery in Guadalajara, Jalisco, Mexico. His parents wanted him to be a priest, but he ran away. He was well educated—he would take in children and teach them in their home in Vulture. My grandfather was a jack-of-all-trades.

My mother met my father in Tucson. When she was about twelve years old, her mother died, and her father brought her and her sisters to Tucson to live with their aunt and godmother, Carmelita Serón. Doña Carmelita had been married to a famous Indian fighter named Hutton. She had lived in the fort and had become friends with the Apaches Manzos. They baptized the children of the Apaches Manzos, and the Indian women would bring her gifts. She was very well off until her husband was killed. I actually remember seeing her—she was very old and very short, and she always wore a *tapalito,* a head covering. My mother attended

Brand of Marcela Rodríguez
(Paternal Grandmother)

St. Augustine Cathedral School until she was sixteen years old, and then she went to work as a seamstress with her cousin, the daughter of Tía Carmelita.

My mother went to school until the sixth grade. She was more educated than a lot of people at that time. She could speak English fluently, as well as Spanish. She could also read and understand Latin—her father had instructed her. She had a lot of books that she read, and she passed on her love of reading to us. I've always loved to read, and when I was in school, I'd always get books from the library. Mother loved Western novels by Zane Grey and Harold Bell Wright. Most of her books were ruined when she left them with her in-laws—they didn't value them. Some of the books had belonged to her father, and I have saved one of her favorites. It is a book of poems and stories by Henry Wadsworth Longfellow. She used to keep it in a trunk wrapped in cloth.

My mother and father met because their families knew each other. My mother and father were married on May 9, 1902, at St. Augustine Cathedral. They celebrated their fiftieth anniversary there!

I was only about three years old when my father sold the ranch near Campbell and River Road, so I don't remember too much except family stories. I do remember the house—it was made of lumber and had only two rooms. And I remember going to a baptism fiesta with my grandmother Marcela and one of my sisters. We came from town in a one-horse buggy—it was a long trip! The fiesta was at the Kennedy Ranch on River Road. They were a Mexican family also. There was music and dancing and lots of cowboys! Another Mexican family who ranched near my parents' home were Benino and Margarita García. There was also a black man named Federico who farmed nearby, and he'd go to town and sell vegetables. My mother would trade tortillas or beef for vegetables, so we always had a lot of vegetables to eat, whether we liked it or not!

It was a hard life. When they were living on the ranch, my mother was having a family, and they were very poor. My mother was not used to the ranch life. When they lived in Wickenburg, they even had someone who washed and ironed for them. On the ranch she had to get the water from a well and wash with a washboard. People say, *"Que bonita la vida del rancho"* [How nice life on the ranch is]. Yes, it is nice, but it is hard!

Brand of Francisco Rodríguez
(Father)

Wedding portrait of Francisco Valencia Rodríguez and María Antonia Parra, St. Augustine Cathedral (May 9, 1902).

Unlike my mother, my father never went to school. He only knew how to write his name. He was a cowboy, and I remember a lot of old-timers like my father who were cowboys—once they got off their horses, they didn't seem to have interest in much of anything. *"¡Ay! ¡Ese caballito!"* my mother used to sigh. "Oh, that horse!"

My older brothers and sisters went to school at Amphitheater in a one-horse buggy. There was a big old mesquite tree in front of the school in those years—if you pass by, you will see that it is still there. One time my father went to the school, and there was a lot of excitement because there was a pig in the classroom. He got there just in time! My father used to go up to the Santa Catalina Mountains to round up cattle, and he used to take a Christmas tree to the school from the mountains during Christmas.

My father told me about a man in the Catalinas who killed mountain lions. He was paid five dollars by the ranchers for every one he killed because the lions would kill their calves. One time my father met up with this man who was camping and frying meat, and, as was the custom in those days, one offered coffee or beans or whatever there was when someone came by. The man offered my father the meat he was cooking, and it was mountain lion meat! My father said it was very good. As the *dicho* says, *"Cuando hay hambre, no hay mal pan!"* [When one is hungry, there is no such thing as bad bread!].

When my father sold the ranch near River and Campbell, we moved into town to Barrio Anita, and I went to Davis School. Our house was right across the street from Davis School—it is still there. When I was about eleven years old, we moved over to Eleventh Avenue, between Fourth and Third Street. I went to catechism at Holy Family Church and made my First Communion there. Then I went to Roskruge and finished the eighth grade, but I never went to high school because we were too poor, and I had to go to work. I started working at the F. H. Keddington Print Shop with my sister Antonia. We stitched booklets and punched out notebooks and sewed books together. We worked on the University of Arizona as well as Tucson High School yearbooks! When the bindery burned down, I worked for the WPA [Works Progress Administration] at making plain dresses to distribute to poor women. Later I moved to Oury Park, where I was in charge of teaching crafts and hobbies to the neighborhood girls. I worked there until I married my husband, Roberto Sotomayor, in 1938.

I remember that when my sister and I worked at the Keddington bindery, we'd walk home for lunch in the summer, and I'd come in all perspired, and mother would have lunch ready for us—coffee, a pot of beans, tortillas, a big kettle of *cocido,* vegetable soup. I'd see her there with that wood stove, and I'd ask myself, "Gosh, how does she do it?" She was a very hard worker and raised us the best she could. She was the one who was in charge of the discipline. She taught us the right values and how to be independent and look after ourselves. She was very well respected. My father was, too, but he was not too involved with us kids. He was very humble and not a go-getter.

My father bought another ranch—thirty acres about thirty miles from town on an old road going out to the Silverbell Mine. He collected firewood to sell on a wagon drawn by a horse and a mule called Susie. We lived in town, and he would go out to the ranch for two weeks at a time, returning to town with a full load of

Francisco Valencia Rodríguez at his ranch in the Silverbell Mountains west of Tucson (ca. 1920).

Roberto Sotomayor, Sr.
(ca. 1925).

wood, which my brothers helped him sell. He also planted corn and watermelons and other crops, which he grew for our family as well as sold. In those days they would prepare the soil and make furrows and then wait for it to rain. It would always rain by June or July, and in August he had a big crop.

When school was out in the summer, we'd go on a rough trail over the Tucson Mountains out to the ranch on the horse-drawn wagon and stay until school started again. We had a small house there. We would run around barefoot in the desert and entertain ourselves. It was very different back then! There was no TV or video games! We'd get big empty lard cans and fill them with water and pour water into the nests of tarantulas to make them crawl out. We'd try to see who could kill the most. But we didn't get them all! At night we slept on canvas cots out in the open with the legs of our cots in cans of water so that the tarantulas could not crawl up on the cots at night! My father would soak cow pies with kerosene and light them to keep the mosquitoes away!

When Roberto and I were married in 1938, we had a civil ceremony because we were poor, and later on we got married in the church. Roberto's family and my family were old-timers and knew each other when they were young. After Roberto's mother died in 1921, his father, Manuel, took his children to California, and Roberto didn't come back until 1936. He was nine years older than I, and I was only eight years old the last time I had seen him! My best friend, Nacha, and her boyfriend arranged for us to meet at midnight mass at Holy Family Church, but my sister Chata had died in March, and I was still sad and didn't feel like going. They practically had to drag me! On New Year's Roberto came to the house to visit, and we started going together. We didn't go out much—we'd visit or go to the show at the Fox and then to the French Café for coffee and cake. Roberto wasn't much for dancing, but that's what I loved the most. My mother was very strict, and if I went to the dances, I'd have to go with my brother or cousin. We'd dance at people's houses or at the Women's Club or the Blue Moon or the Riverside—it was nice then. But the best dancing was at the Wetmore!

After we were married, Roberto bought a lot on the south side and built a one-room house; we called it the garage. Then he bought another lot and built me a bigger house on Colombia Street in the Government Heights neighborhood. He enlarged the "garage" and rented it. Roberto was always a very responsible man when it came to taking care of his family. He was always looking to the future—he was a good businessman. When he made a deal, he knew how he was going to pay.

Roberto's family was a pioneer family that came from Hermosillo in the mid-1800s and homesteaded in the area that is now surrounded by Ina Road, La Cholla Boulevard, and Jayne's Station Road. Roberto's father and uncle, Manuel and Florencio, were the original homesteaders. Manuel ran cattle here above Jayne's Station Road, and Florencio farmed down below, across the road. Florencio raised chile, tomato, squash, beans, and corn. When Florencio got sick, Manuel bought his share and farmed also—he raised hay and alfalfa for his cattle. My husband, Roberto, was born in 1905 in a little adobe house that his father Manuel built next to a large arroyo not far from here. Later they built a larger adobe dwelling that became the "rancho."

Even when we lived in town, Roberto was interested in the ranch. He used to come out here and help his father, Don Manuel. When I first came out here, Don Manuel was still alive, and there were still the old mesquite *retaque* corrals, a well,

Brand of Manuel Sotomayor
(Father-in-law)

Sotomayor adobe built in the early 1900s in northwest Tucson, at La Cholla Boulevard and Jayne's Station Road (ca. 1950).

Carlotta Sotomayor with
portraits of her husband's
parents and grandparents in
the bedroom of her former
home in northwest Tucson.
Photo by José Galvez (2000).

and a windmill. He still used a horse-drawn wagon, and I saved a couple of the wooden wheels, which I have out in front of the house.

When Don Manuel died in 1946, Roberto bought his brothers' shares in the ranch. They were not interested in the ranch life, as Roberto was. We moved out to the ranch from town in January of 1950. We already had six children—one of our daughters was only six months old. Although I was born on my parents' homestead, I was raised in town, and I didn't know too much about ranch life. It was hard at first. I raised ten children in that little adobe house that Roberto's father built. It had two bedrooms—one for the boys and one for the girls. At first I washed outside in a tub and had to heat the water with a wood fire. I used to pull the table in the kitchen away from the wall so we could eat and then push it back so I could let down the ironing board to iron! But I think back, and I say to myself, "I did okay in that little house!"

Roberto always had another job when we had the ranch. After he lost his job with the Southern Pacific, he went to work for a construction company that was building houses in the Catalina Foothills. He helped build a stone house there, and he liked it so much that he asked the foreman if he could have some rocks; the foreman told him he could have all the rocks that he wanted. So every day he'd bring home a load of rocks, and that is what this house I'm living in now is built of. A man named Mr. Romero and his three sons built this house in 1961, but Roberto did the carpentry and most of the inside work. Roberto sold the eighty acres across Jayne's Station Road, and we used the money to build this house on the hill overlooking the old ranch. It has five bedrooms. I used to get lost going from room to room! In 1961, when we moved in, we were even on a national television commercial for Armstrong Tile Company!

At one time there were corrals down below, and Roberto built a slaughterhouse. He ran about fifty head of cattle. Ranch life was hard on our sons because they were in school, and they had to do all the chores outside. They took care of the animals; they fed the cattle, hogs, and chickens and worked long hours in the fields. The boys would gather the corn stalks, and Roberto bought a grinder to grind the stalks for feed. My boys raised pigs. When our oldest son, Roberto (Bobby), went to Amphi, he bought some chicks and raised fryers. I used to kill and clean and cook them—three and four at a time. Our three boys were in Future Farmers

Brand of Roberto Sotomayor
(Husband)

of America—they raised pigs and cattle and grew squash and chile and took them to the State Fair. In Phoenix they brought home first, second, and third prizes. We'd make the red chile *ristras* [dried chile strung on a string], and I'd say, "Where's MY ribbon?"

I would dry squash and *chicos* [tender corn kernels). We made *carne seca*. I would cut the meat in strips and put salt and pepper and garlic on it, and Roberto would hang it in the slaughterhouse. Before he built the slaughterhouse, I would hang the meat on the clothesline—you have to keep turning it so that it will dry. This was when I was living in the little adobe house down below.

Roberto would milk the cows, and if there was plenty of milk, I would make cheese. I didn't like using the *cuajo* [curd] for a starter, so I bought little tablets of rennet. Roberto used to sell or give all my cheese away, and I used to get mad and tell him, "I'm not going to make anymore cheese. If you sell the cheese, then give me the money because I am the maker of the cheese!" And I'd keep a gallon or two of milk in the refrigerator and settle the cream. I'd make butter just for the family.

Roberto used to plant from here all the way to the house you can see across the way. He planted watermelons, corn, squash, tomatoes, and green chile. People loved the *chile verde* we grew—we were famous for that! The boys did the heavy work—the only time I went into the milpa was to pick the chile and sometimes to keep an eye on the water. My father-in-law, Don Manuel, used to tell us women that if we were pregnant, we shouldn't go into the fields because they would dry up. I used to tell my sister-in-law, "Better for us!" We used to laugh!

When they'd go into the fields, my son Bobby would drive a tractor, and they'd fill the wagon with cornstalks and bring in the watermelons or corn or whatever was harvested. Bobby and Dickey, my third child, were Roberto's labor force. In October, when the weather was starting to change, they'd bring in the squash and red chile, and Roberto would cover them with a canvas so they wouldn't rot. He'd sell some to Jerry's Lee Ho Market down there on south Main as well as to other Chinese grocery stores. Much was also sold here at the ranch to drive-up customers.

During the time that Roberto was raising cattle, his older brother came to visit from California. He told Roberto, "Brother, make me a *barbacoa*." Well, Roberto

Sotomayor children in the milpa at the Sotomayor ranch in northwest Tucson, at La Cholla Boulevard and Jayne's Station Road (ca. 1950s).

got enthused, and the other brothers came, and they started to work. They made a ramada down below and dug a pit. They made a bar. They cut cornstalks and tied them with wire and put them on the west side of the ramada for shade. They smelled very pretty. By Sunday it was ready. Roberto barbecued a steer in the pit. We had musicians. We had beer. Nothing was lacking. My sisters came to help me make tortillas—oh, my Lord, all the tortillas we made! I cooked a huge drum of frijoles. I made rice. My sisters helped me make salsa. The word got out—people came that we didn't even know. I think about five hundred people came to that fiesta! I don't know how I survived—I got a fever that day! Anyway, I made it!

We have had a lot of family gatherings here on this land—special occasions like weddings, baptisms, and holidays. In 1995 we had a reunion of the Rodríguez branch of the family. I am the matriarch now. The reunion included the Sotomayores, the Gómezes, the Castaños, the Nuñezes, and the Acedos—*toda la*

Carlotta Parra Rodríguez Sotomayor *(right)* and her sister Dolores Rodríguez Mendoza making tortillas at a wood stove for a family fiesta at the Sotomayor ranch in northwest Tucson.

familia. There were five generations here, about three hundred people, counting the little ones. There were children all over–about one hundred children. We held the reunion down by the old adobe house at the bottom of the hill that my husband, Roberto, was raised in. One of my nephews, who is an electrician, connected the lights from the water pump on the well. We put up three or four canvases, so we had a lot of shade. We had a live band, and there was a big concrete slab that we used for dancing. We had it catered this time! Barbecue, beans, salsa, rice, and tortillas. My sisters-in-law made the salsa, and I made the *teswín* [a fermented corn drink]. There were piñatas before sundown–one for the children and one for the grownups. That's when the fun really began! That was the last big party that we had!

Roberto retired in 1962, and we started traveling with friends or our children. We went to Mexico and Europe and traveled to different areas of the United States. He started taking care of some apartments that we had. He was always working; he couldn't sit still! He was a very intelligent man, and when he had a problem, he wouldn't give up until he solved it! He had big hands, and he used to say, "My hands are my tools." The only thing is, he didn't like to read. The only thing he read was the newspaper. He was just too hyper!

Roberto died in 1992 at the age of eighty-six. He passed away here at his beloved rancho. He was born and raised on this land, and this is where he wanted to die. Before he died, he wanted to sell the rest of the land and knock down the house because he didn't wanted anybody else living in it.

Some of the original homestead had to be sold during the depression because they couldn't pay the taxes, but this part was saved—all the way up to La Cholla Boulevard. A few years ago Roberto's sister's sons sold the last five acres across from the Northwest Hospital. His sister had about twenty-five acres, and each child got five acres.

I feel bad about it, but I think that it's best that I sell, too. Some of my kids feel bad about it. Some people say, "But what about the rancho?" But it's not a rancho anymore. It's just a house, and the house is too big for me and Carmen, my daughter who lives with me. It is expensive to keep up with the taxes and all.

We are trying to get the property rezoned—hopefully by July and then through the Pima County Board of Supervisors. Up here they will allow two houses per acre and down below three houses per acre, but they keep changing things. The big stone house that I'm living in will be fixed up and sold—at least that's what the developer tells me. As far as we know, the old adobe house that Don Manuel built and that Roberto was raised in will be torn down. I feel sad about that. I wish they would preserve it for many more years.

It is very hard after fifty-five years of living here. At my age it is hard to move, but I have to go with the change. One time my grandson asked me what I was doing sitting on the porch all alone, and I said, "I'm just sitting here looking at the sky, thinking back about the years that have gone by, the things we did, the things we didn't do. How all my kids and family were all over here at one time." It used to be so pretty here, so quiet with so much open space. I was sitting by myself seeing how the town has grown and how big Tucson is now. We didn't used to see any cars going by. Now it's like a freeway. We didn't used to see any lights at night. Now I open my windows and blinds, and I can't see very well because of the glare from that Target and that K-Mart on Ina that are open all night. I'm not sure what I'll do when I move. Maybe I'll buy a small house or condo.

Savoring the last few months at her former home, Carlotta Sotomayor will soon leave the ranch property that has long since left Sotomayor hands. Photo by José Galvez (2000).

I had heard of the Sotomayor family homestead for many years through members of their family and was finally introduced to Mrs. Carlotta Sotomayor through a mutual friend, Irma J. Sotomayor Moreno. The first interviews took place in 1997 and 1998, and I continued gathering information from family albums and photographs over the next few years. My last interview for the purposes of this book was in the fall of 2002, but I continue to make personal visits. The property was rezoned, and in 1998 the remaining twenty-three acres of the Sotomayor homestead were sold to a developer who has built about sixty houses on the property. The small adobe house where Carlotta raised her young family and where her husband, Roberto, had also been raised, was demolished. The developer also tore down the large stone house Roberto built in the 1960s for his growing family; he thought it would be too expensive to renovate. Mrs. Sotomayor bought a small single-family home in a development just north of the Foothills Mall in Northwest Tucson, where she lives with her daughter, Carmen.

Carlotta Sotomayor, her daughters Carmen and Rosemary, her son Rene, and his son Rene Jr. stand beneath one of the street signs with their family names at the housing development the Sotomayor Ranch. The whole area was once their family ranch in northwest Tucson.

Ramona Franco reads the
Bible in front of her home altar
in her Barrio Viejo home.
Photo by José Galvez (1995).

Ramona Benítez Franco

I was born on the thirteenth of May 1902, on my parents' ranch in the Rincon Mountains. My parents' names were Angel Benítez and Desideria Vindiola. My father was born in Banamachi, Sonora, Mexico, in 1860 and died in 1937. He came to Tucson at the age of nine with his parents and his sisters. My paternal grandparents' names were Jesús Benítez and Felisa Cisneros. When my father's mother died, his father returned to Mexico–he had a vineyard there. My father stayed in Tucson with Pedro and Elena Pellón, who later became my god-parents. My father was raised by them in a large brick house that is still standing on Simpson Street. My father began to work as a very young boy; Mr. Pellón had freight wagons, and my father was responsible for watering the horses.

Speaking of my godparents, my *ninos* were good friends with the bishop, and when I was baptized, my ninos Pellón recited a very old prayer that he taught them. No one else I know had this prayer when they were baptized!

Reciban esta niña
De que de la iglesia salió
Con los santos sacramentos
Y el agua que recibió.

Te recibimos con gusto
De que la iglesia saliste
Con los santos sacramentos
Y el agua que recibiste.

Receive this child
As she departs from the church
With the holy sacraments
And the holy water she has received.

*Brand of Gabriel Vindiola
(Maternal Grandfather)*

We receive you with joy
On your departure from the church
With the holy sacraments
And the holy water you have received.

My mother was born in Ures, Sonora, Mexico, in 1873 and died in 1936. She came to Tucson as a very young girl with her parents, María Leyvas and Gabriel Vindiola. They lived at one time close to the family Pellón, and my father used to tell my godfather, "I sure do like that girl, Pedro." And Pedro would say, "She is too young for you, Angel." Much later my mother and father became acquainted, and they were married on September 15, 1888, in the old St. Augustine Cathedral, which was located in what is now La Placita Village.

I still have the letter that my father wrote to my mother's father asking for her hand in marriage and my grandfather's reply:

Tucsón, Agosto 29, 1887
    M. Señor Don Gabriel Bindiola: Muy Señor Mío:
    Tengo el honor de dirigir la presente que lleva por objeto de comunicarle que, contando con la voluntad de Desideria, pido a Ud. la mano de ella para esposa. Deseando la atención de Ud. quedo en espera de su contesta.
    Su atento y seguro servidor, Angel Benítes

Tucsón, Agosto 31.
    Sr. Don Angel Benítes: Muy Señor Mío:
    He recibido su carta de Ud. Fecha 29 y he consultado con mi hija y me ha contestado de acuerdo con las pretensiones de. Ud. De manera que ella de los pasos que le convengan.
    De afectísimo y seguro servidor, Gabriel Bindiola

Tucson, August 29, 1887
    My most esteemed Don Gabriel Vindiola:
    I have the honor of sending to you this letter that I have written with the purpose of communicating to you that if Desideria is in agreement, I ask for your permission to take her hand in marriage. Thank you for the attention to this matter. I wait anxiously for your reply.
    Your attentive and faithful servant, Angel Benítez

Señor Don Angel Benítez: My dear Sir:

I have received your letter on the 31st, and I have consulted with my daughter. She has agreed to your request for her hand in marriage. In that case she may make the plans that are convenient to her.

Your most affectionate and faithful servant, Gabriel Vindiola.

After they were married, my father bought a few head of cattle and leased some land in the area of San Xavier Mission that was called Los Reales. My oldest brother, Angel, and my sisters Teresa (Yichi) and María (Yita) were born on that ranch. There were nine children altogether—the rest of us, Felisa (Chula), Rosario (Nina), myself (Chocha), Ignacia (Nacia), Guadalupe (Ruby), and Juan were born on the ranch in the Rincon Mountains.

By that time my maternal grandparents, "Ma María" and "Pa Biel," had a homestead in "El Rincón"; they were among the first people who settled there. When my grandfather found out that there was some land available, he told my father, and my father bought about 140 acres and began to buy more cattle. He built corrals and built an adobe house, and that is how the ranch was made. He started out with ten calves, and they kept increasing, and that is how he built his herd.

I remember my maternal grandparents very well. Their ranch was close to ours. There was a small hill close to our ranch, and on the other side of that hill was the ranch of my grandparents. There was a path on that hill, and I used to go over it on foot to visit Pa Biel and Ma María. I used to spend a lot of time with them and even would spend the night, sleeping between the two of them.

My grandmother, Ma María, used to have a vigil for the Santo Niño de Atocha every year. She would sing the songs of praise, and I would sing with her. That is why I still remember all the verses by heart:

Celebre todos cristianos
Ante tus pasos divinos
Y con tus poderosas manos
Nos prestarás tu auxilio.

Angel Benítez and Desideria
Vindiola Benítez with children
Rosario and Juan (ca. 1910).

Divino Jesús
En tu dulce nombre
Con tu eterna luz
Se ilumine el hombre.
(Etc.)

May all Christians
Celebrate your Divine Way.
Because with your powerful hands
You aid us.

Divine Jesus
Oh, Sweet Name!
Your divine light
Lights our way.
(Etc.)

When my grandmother had her vigil to honor the Santo Niño, all the ranchers would attend because the people out on the ranches in those days, the people who lived on the ranches, were very Catholic–more so than the people in town, I think. There were a lot of people who attended the vigils so that they could pay their *mandas*–their promises. Every ranch had its own *velorio,* and we would go to all of them. They would honor different saints–San José, la Virgen del Carmen, la Virgen del Refugio, and San Isidro, the patron saint of farmers. From the time they were married, my parents never failed to have a vigil to honor the Virgen de Guadalupe. The statue of the Virgen was decorated first thing in the morning. They made an altar with sheets and curtains that were hung around on the walls and from the ceiling, and then they would place flowers on the altar. Old and young would pray and sing together, and all the ranchers would remove their sombreros out of respect.

En una virtuosa nube
Me causó mucha alegría
Y en un arco de color
Vi a la virgen María.

Juan Diego quedó elevado
De que tan linda que la veía
Lo llamó y subió a la cuesta
A ver lo que quería.
(Etc.)

A virtuous cloud
Caused me much joy
And on a rainbow
I saw the Virgin Mary.

Juan Diego was transported
By the beautiful vision
And climbed the hill
To find out what her wishes were.
Etc.

During the vigil for the Virgen de Guadalupe, whose feast day is December 12, they would begin the rosary by singing "Ave María Purísima." I used to love that because it seemed to me that it was at that moment that the devil fled! After reciting the rosary, they sang the *alabanzas* [songs of praise], and the people in attendance would stay until dawn of the next day and wouldn't leave until after they had had breakfast!

I have the painting of the Virgen de Guadalupe that belonged to my parents on my home altar here at my house. My sister Chula [Felisa] and I used to have the velorio for the Virgen de Guadalupe like the one our parents had at the ranch. She would come and help me decorate and fix the altar. But I haven't had a velorio since my sister died, and I have never taken down the Virgen from my altar since the day she died.

I will never forget one Christmas that it snowed. I remember feeling sorry for all the horses out in the cold in the corrals! They put up a big tent. Everyone had gotten together to wait for the Baby Jesus. They had a little cradle for him. They made an altar with all the saints, but they didn't put the Baby Jesus out until midnight, the morning of the twenty-fifth. Manuela—we called her Milela—my mother's paternal aunt, was living for a time on my grandfather Gabriel's ranch. How that little old lady could sing! One Christmas she invited the Yaqui Matachines out to the ranch to dance. They wore costumes and masks and carried poles all decorated with ribbons. It was the only time I ever saw that fiesta! A lot of ranchers came to that Christmas velorio, and it snowed that very night. When midnight arrived, all the *viejitos* [elders] began to sing:

Una tropa de gitanos
Vienen a adorar el niño
Vienen a mecer su cuna
Arru, ro, ro, ro

A band of gypsies
Come to adore the Christ Child
They have come to rock his cradle
A la ro, ro, ro

Ramona Benítez (Franco) *(left)*
and sister Felisa Benítez
(Franco) (ca. 1915).

And then the grown men adored the Christ Child:

Arrullan los hombres
Al Niño Jesús
Que les dio su gracia
Y también su luz
Arru, a la ro, ro, ro.

Men sing
The Christ Child to sleep
He filled us with his grace
And his light.
A la ro, ro, ro.

    As I said, the people on the ranches in those days were very religious. My father always saw to it that we arose every morning with a prayer:

Con Dios me acuesto
Con Dios me levanto
Con la gracia de Dios
Y el Espíritu Santo
Dios contigo
Yo con él
Dios delante
Y yo tras él.

I lie down with Christ
I arise with Christ
By the grace of God
And the Holy Ghost.
May God be with you
And also with me.
God leads the way
And I follow Him.

    And my mother even taught me and my cousin Quirino Montoya our *doctrina*. We were sick with the measles and couldn't come into town for our catechism. Just before we were to make our First Communion, she brought us into town for the practice. The priest told her that he could not allow us to make our First Communion because the nuns had not instructed us. I remember crying. And then Mother told the priest, "If you will test the children on their prayers and doctrina, and if they do not know it well enough, I will be in agreement." When the priest tested us, he was surprised, and he told Mother, "These children know their prayers and catechism better than the ones who were instructed in town!"

They made a lot of food for the velorios—enchiladas, tamales, *carne con chile colorado* [meat with red chile], *carne frita* [fried meat], *carne blanca*. Carne blanca is now called *carne a la mexicana*—it is made with tomato, onion, and green chile. The women made large amounts of delicious soft tortillas—not like the truck tires that you buy today! The store-bought tortillas are the reason so many people suffer nowadays from *empacho*—indigestion!

Doña Bernarda Téllez, my brother Angel's mother-in-law, held the velorio for San Isidro. In the times of drought and little rain all the ranchers would gather in procession through the fields carrying the statue of San Isidro. Everyone prayed the rosary and sang the alabanzas:

Señor San Isidro
Niño Labrador
Ruégale al Señor
Por el pecador.

Señor San Isidro
De Dios tan querido
Pues en tu labor
Seáis mi padrino.

Los ángeles todos
Que le amparaban
La Virgen María
Las gracias les daba.
(Etc.)

Dearest St. Isidro
Child Laborer
Pray to God
For us sinners.

Ramona Benítez Franco's sister
María at her First Communion
(May 19, 1916).

Saint Isidro
Beloved of God
Because of your labors
You are my godfather.

All the angels
That came to your aid
Were given grace
By the Virgin Mary.
(Etc.)

When they held the vigil for la Virgen del Carmen, they prayed:

La Virgen del Carmen
Es nuestra protectora
Con tal auxilio
No hay de temer.
Vence al mundo
De todo pecado
Y guerra contra Lucifer.

The Virgin of Mt. Carmel
Is our protectress;
Because of her intercession
We have nothing to fear.
She is victorious over all sin
In the world;
She wages wars against Lucifer.

And to los Dulces Nombres [the Holy Names, the Holy Family] they prayed:

Jesús, José y María,
Os doy el corazón
Y el alma mía.
Jesús, José y María,

Asístanme en mi última agonía
Jesús, José y María,
Que muera en paz
En su dulce compañía.

Jesus, Mary, and Joseph,
I give you my heart
And my soul.
Jesus, Joseph, and Mary
Help me in my final agony!
Jesus, Joseph, and Mary,
Grant that I might die in peace
In your sweet company!

And I know it's hard to believe, but here in this house that I'm living in now, my grandmother, Ma María, died praying with that very prayer on her lips. She was already very sick, and they went to bring the priest, and my mother asked her, "What do you want, Mother?" "I want to give everyone my final *bendición,*" she said. The family was around her, and she gave us her blessing and said, "Ay, ay, ay." We brought out the alcohol, and we were massaging her, and she died in that very moment.

My parents and my grandparents' ranch house was made of adobe. They made the houses themselves without a plan, and they were very similar. When my father made the adobes for our house, a big hole was left [in the ground], and so when it rained, it filled with water as if it were a pond! When you entered our house, there was a big hall and a very large kitchen with a fireplace to one side. The living room, which also had a fireplace, was on the other side of the hall, and in the back there were two bedrooms. The living room also had a fireplace, where a clock with chimes was hung. And I know it's hard to believe, but when the cathedral bells chimed in town, we could hear them all the way out to our house on the ranch. And that clock never lost time!

From the wide hallway you could pass out to the backyard, where there was a big ramada, and to one side of the ramada, attached to the house, was another room that was used as a storeroom. Behind the house were a well and the windmill that pumped water and also the corral for the cows and the *canoas* [troughs], which were filled with water for the cows to drink. To one side of the well was the big *tanque* for the cattle, and the windmill would go all day and night, pouring water into that tank because my father had a lot of cattle. And also behind the house there was a flower garden. My oldest sister, Teresa–Yichi–had a green thumb; she had so many beautiful flowers! And close to the corral where we had the milk cows, Mother had a fence around an orchard where she had peach and apricot trees, and in the rows between the trees she grew corn, green beans, tomatoes, radishes, green chile, and *chile de pájaro*. If you wanted good chile, come to my mother and father's ranch!

I'm going to tell you something–maybe you won't believe me! Whether it was someone's saint's day or a Sunday, or just someone coming to visit, all the families would get together, and whoever knew how to play the guitar played and sang. Wherever one went, there were dances. The people were very happy, very united. My grandfather Pa Biel and Don Dionisio Téllez–they were very old– would get brooms and pretend they were guitars! They would start to sing, and the people would dance! I especially remember Manuel Escalante. When he played the guitar, he would put one foot on a chair and sing the song "Trigueña Hermosa." Because we were seven daughters, there were always suitors and a fiesta going on at our house! That's why I say we were so happy and comfortable in those days.

My father knew a lot of fairy tales. In the winter season when it was cold, many of the ranchers would come to our house and sit in front of the fireplace and listen to my father tell his stories. They'd make coals in the fireplace and would grill meat and make peanut brittle! The house was always full of people. People came from town and stayed at our ranch when they went to hunt because our ranch was on the road to the mountains. It was very beautiful there because Rincon Creek flowed not too far away from our house. My father never hunted very much, however. Once in a while he would shoot a rabbit, and we would cook it on the grill. I remember once that the Escalante brothers–they called them Los Chanavelos–killed a mountain lion, and they brought the meat to the ranch, but my mother did not want to eat it because the meat was very white, and she was afraid of it!

Gathering of family and friends at the Benítez ranch in the Rincon Mountains east of Tucson (ca. 1910).

My mother taught us how to eat everything; she was a very good cook. We ate grilled meat, and she made *albóndigas* [meatballs] with ground meat. When they killed a beef, they would make *carne seca*–they hung the meat on long thick wires, and they would put curtains of cheesecloth on it to keep the flies off. When the coals were ready, we would put strips of dried meat on the coals. Oh, how delicious the fat smelled! Nowadays no one eats lard because they say it is bad for you, but I was born eating lard, and I have never stopped eating it! Mother made *caldo puchero,* also called *cocido.* It is a soup made with beef bones and vegetables. She also made a soup with the carne seca that is called *casuela* and a delicious soup with tepary beans. She cooked red chile with cheese and potatoes, *pozole* with bones or meat, milk tripe, liver, and a soup with *librillo* [part of the cow stomach that has "leaves" that resemble a "booklet"], which nowadays they throw away.

My mother also made *queso asadero* [cooked cheese], *requesón* [cottage cheese], and butter. Father would take mother's cheeses to sell where the train stopped in Vail and also into town. She had a *batea* [wooden mixing bowl] where she made yeast bread and biscuits. She would make the dough at night, and by the morning it had risen. We would take the bread for lunch when we went to school. Oh, how delicious it was! Mother also made tortillas, of course. The *gorditas*–they would rise so much that it seemed that they were two tortillas together! Mother also raised chickens, and many people came to the ranch to buy her fryers and eggs.

We helped Mother around the house. We washed, ironed, and cooked. Our mother made all of our clothes. My sisters Yichi and Chula were very good at sewing and embroidering. Mother was very good at crocheting and knitting. I have saved some of the crocheted things that Mother made. I remember Mother crocheting in the evening when the day's work was done, and if she happened to run out of thread, she would use the string from the sacks of flour! (I liked to embroider, too, and many years later, when my sons were small and quarantined with scarlet fever, I made them embroider dishtowels and pillowcases to pass the time away!) I still have some of mother's dishes and the napkins with crocheted trim and the embroidered tablecloth that she used to put on our table at the ranch. It was a very big homemade table, and we would sit on benches. When we would sit down to eat, she would serve the little ones first, then my father, and then she would eat.

We played *"comadres"* ["house"] with our dolls and furniture. We had everything–little beds, tables, and even miniature wood-burning stoves that looked like the real thing. We had dishes that looked exactly like the ones our mother used! Father bought them for us in town at a store called La Pagoda.

Except for the three oldest children, we were all born out there on the ranch with the same midwife. Her name was Doña Bruna Vilducea. She came on horseback from the Tanque Verde area. She had her midwife license. She died here in town when she was very ancient–on Convent Street. When she was attending to my mother, she would arrive with a suitcase, and she would tell us, "Don't touch the suitcase, *mijita,* because it has a little boy doll or girl doll in it, and if you touch it, it will fall apart!" Well, I would keep going by the suitcase, wanting to see inside because I wanted that doll, but I never did! I never knew when Mother was expecting a child–I only found out when the baby was born! Oh, the innocence of those times! The people back then were very reserved–they didn't open the eyes of young children to anything!

For a time when I was growing up, Señorita Carmen Téllez was the teacher; she taught in her home on her parents' ranch. I think she must have gone to school in Tucson because she knew English. No one wanted to go out there to teach because it was so far from town. Then my father began to insist that there be a school out in the Rincon Valley, and he went around collecting signatures, and finally a school was built. It was about a mile from our house, and we would go to school in a horse-drawn buggy. One of the teachers that I had was named Ora McCannus. She and her mother lived for a time with us in a room on our ranch. They were so good–they were like family. Another teacher that I remember was named Mr. Phillips; he was very good also.

A rancher who owns his own ranch is always busy with one kind of business or another. He has to see to it that his horses and cattle have good pasture; he has to see to the fences and make sure that the cattle are not sick or injured. Father would deliver calves in May and October, and at times he would sell 130 to 140 head and sometimes more. Buyers would come out to the ranch from Tucson, and they would pick out the calves they wanted, and then they would drive the calves all the way into town to the Twenty-ninth Street stockyard, where they would be corralled. My father also had cattle grazing up in the mountains, and he would go up to the mountain pastures and drive the cattle down to our ranch. As the saying goes, *"Un solo res que sigue a su camino, no le hace que tan bronco, lo siguen los demás"* [If one good cow follows the right path, it doesn't matter how wild the others are; they will follow him]! There is also a *dicho, "Una res mala alborata a todo el pueblo"* [A bad cow can influence the whole herd].

Father also owned land alongside the Pantano River, and he irrigated all that milpa with the rains that came from the heavens. That's how all the farmers in the area raised their crops in those days. The arroyo was named Rincon Creek, and the water ran clear and beautiful. Father harvested beans, corn, pumpkins, squash, watermelon, and cantaloupe, which he sold in town. We would also gather *verdolagas* [purslane] during the rainy season in July and August, and he would put them in big sacks and deliver them to the stores. He also raised alfalfa, and when the alfalfa dried, he used machinery to cut and pack it. My father had a lot of modern machinery on the ranch; in fact, many of the other ranchers would often borrow it. Father was always very generous. During the harvest season about twenty-five men would come from town to help him, and he always provided them with board, food, and a salary. They would tell him, "Don Lito, when you need help, come for us."

Brand of Manuel Benítez
(Uncle)

There were a lot of Mexican ranchers in the Rincon Mountains in those days. Behind us were the Ruizes, the Méndezes, Fulgencio Molina, Chico Téllez, and the Duartes. Señor Ruiz was very rich. It was said that he buried his gold in a ten-gallon lard can! People used call the Duartes *"los ratones"* because they always arrived at dinnertime! A couple of ranches that were higher in the mountains were the ranches of Tomás Mills and Isolde Mills; they were Mexican even though they had the name Mills. Alberto Franco had a small ranch, and the Barceló family had a small ranch also in the foothills. They had a very well-built and pretty house. Tío Eusebio, who was the brother of my grandmother, Ma María, also had a ranch, which was close to theirs in the area called "El Cajoncito" because it was in a box canyon. He had a little dam, and when it filled with water, everybody would go to picnic there. They even had little paddle boats that they used in the "lake"!

Like I tell my sons, my father *"no era un ratón de un solo agujero"* [was not a rat with only one hole; that is, he was a jack-of-all-trades]. He did a little bit of everything. He also had lime kilns. He would collect the limestone rocks in the area and cut the wood of the palo verde tree to build the fire in the kiln. When they were burning the limestone, they had to stay at the kiln all night so that the fire would not go out. If the fire went out, the lime would be raw and would not be any good.

I remember so well the wedding of my brother Angel and Bernardita Téllez! She was the daughter of Don Dionisio Téllez and Doña Bernarda Téllez, who also had a ranch in the area. They were married in town at the cathedral, and after the ceremony they came back to the ranch in a buggy with glass windows drawn by two white horses decorated with flowers and feathers on their heads! My father paid for a horse-drawn wagon so that the musicians and all the townspeople invited would have a ride to the ranch! My father slaughtered two steers for the wedding celebration, and they made a barbecue. The musicians played all day and all night. Their instruments were the bass violin, *guitarrón,* and flute. They danced *cuadrillas* [square dances], the schottische, the *varsoviana,* polkas, waltzes, and mazurkas. The dances of yesteryear were so pure—not like the nasty dances of today like *la quebradita!*

My brother Angel was the oldest, and he was the one who helped my father

Brand of Angel Benítez
(Father)

the most with the ranch. After he married Bernardita, the First World War began, and Bernardita said, "Ay! They're going to take my Angelito!" My father said, "No, don't worry, they won't take him." He was not in favor of them fleeing to escape the war, but they decided to go to Mexicali, Mexico, anyway. At that time there was also a great flu epidemic that almost no one survived. Here in this area everyone had to wear masks. My brother Angel got sick in Mexico, and when they let my mother know, she went immediately to Mexicali. "Go ahead and go," my father told her, "and then let me know how he is doing." Because of the epidemic, no one was allowed to cross the border, but my mother crossed anyway on a board plank. It is hard to imagine her doing that because she was so heavy. That's a mother's love for you! Well, my brother did die after all, and my father had such a struggle to bring his body home, as well as his wife and two children, Adalberto and Matilde. He had to pay a lot of money so that they could cross the border. Mr. Steinfeld helped my father by writing dozens of letters of support. He and my father were friends because they had arrived in Tucson at the same time. They had to seal my brother's body in three caskets so that the sickness would not contaminate anyone. My mother had to cross back into the United States illegally again because at that time they were not allowing anyone to cross the border in either direction.

Not long after that, my father broke his shoulder and some ribs when a horse fell on him. My brother Juan was still very young, and my father could no longer manage the ranch alone. He had also gotten into a lot of debt when Angel died in Mexico. He had to pay for two funerals—one in Mexico and one here. It just so happened that there was a bad drought just about that time, and my father had to send his cattle to another ranch for pasture. He was never able to get them back, and so he was finally forced to sell the ranch.

My father bought a house in Tucson on South Eighth Avenue that belonged to the Ruiz family. It is the house I am still living in. It was built in 1902 and is as old as I am. My father then opened a grocery store on the corner of the house—he named it Angel Benítez Grocery, and he made a very good living at it for a while because he sold things very cheaply.

I attended Safford School until the eighth grade. I wanted to help out my parents then, and so I went to work at Rite Way Cleaners, which was located on the corner of Sixth and Congress. I ironed, and I was paid by the hour. My bosses were very pleased with my work. I even washed and ironed the clothes of John Dillinger when he was in town before they arrested him! But I didn't know about it until later! I married Rogelio Franco in 1933. I worked for only two weeks after I got married. My husband, Roy, said to me, "I didn't get married to come home and stare at the ceiling all alone!" We had three sons—Roy, Hector, and Leslie. My husband died in 1963. My son Leslie comes every day from his job in the Water Department and has lunch with me, and my son Roy comes to check on me almost every day because I still live alone in this old house. I tell my sons, "I live with my memories and my saints."

I don't know why I remember so much detail about the old days. I can see our house on the ranch as if it were in front of my eyes. I still remember the names of some of our horses: El Trigueño, El Jardín, Sandy, Portrillo, and Alanza. We called one horse El Jardín because he liked to go into the garden and eat the flowers and vegetables! Jennie was a short mare; Morón, a big mare. I wish I had pictures of the house and the windmill and the canal where the water ran! We left so many of our things on the ranch when we left! There were so many things that we could have saved as keepsakes! I used to have my father's branding iron, AB, in the little shed behind my home but someone stole it!

Now they say that it is very difficult to get to our ranch. Before, from my backyard here it was about fifteen miles going straight up Twenty-second Street and crossing the Pantano Wash. The road was different in those days. Now everything is fenced, and one has to ask permission to enter the area. Before, everything was open and free. They say that where my father's ranch used to be, they have sold lots and are building very elegant houses. Someone has bought our old ranch house and fixed it up, but we can't locate them to find out if we can visit. The family is named Mortensen, but they are not listed in the phonebook.

The last time I went to our ranch was in the 1960s with my niece Jessie, the daughter of my oldest sister, Teresa. The windmill and the well and the gardens and corrals were no longer there. I have a rock on my window sill that I brought from the ranch of my Pa Biel and Ma María the last time I went. It seemed to me to be so pretty! You can see the ruins of their adobe house from the road. I put the date that I was there—the second of April 1967.

Ramona Franco with her son
Leslie within blocks of
downtown Tucson. Photo by
José Galvez (2002).

One-hundred-year-old Ramona Benítez Franco has lived in the same downtown Tucson home since 1917. Photo by José Galvez (2002).

➡️ At a League of Mexican American Women's annual *quinceañera* luncheon, a gentleman came to speak to me after my presentation. "If you are collecting a history of ranches, you need to speak to my *tía* Ramona," Chayo (Rosario) Franco told me. "She grew up on her parents' and grandparents' ranches in the Rincon Mountains east of Tucson. She is in her midnineties, and her memory is still very sharp." I visited Doña Ramona ("Chocha") several times and taped my interviews on September 16 and 22 and October 20, 1994. I had several conversations over *cafecito* with her in the succeeding years, during which she shared family photographs with me and showed me her mother's and grandmother's antique needlework that she has saved in an ancient trunk. I last visited her in the fall of 2002. She still lives alone in her historic adobe house south of Tucson's city center and is visited frequently by her sons and members of her family. In May 2002, family and friends gathered around her, Doña Ramona celebrated her one hundredth birthday with a mass and reception at Santa Cruz Church.

Elena Vásquez Cruz occupies her time crocheting. Photo by José Galvez (2000).

Elena Vásquez Cruz

I was born on December 18, 1912, at El Rancho de los Sosa on the San Pedro River north of Benson, Arizona. My father's name was Victor Escalante Vásquez; he was born in Imurís, Sonora, Mexico, in 1871. My paternal grandparents' names were Narciso Vásquez and Clemente Escalante. The family left Mexico when my father was about five years old. My mother's name was Ramona Isabel López Montijo. My maternal grandparent's names were Juana López and Seráfico Montijo. My mother was born on August 30, 1875, in the Coolidge area while her parents were making their journey from Mexico to the United States.

Life in Mexico was hard, especially for the *peones*. My grandfather, Narciso Vásquez, was hired by the Soto family to work the fields of their big hacienda. He cultivated and irrigated and harvested the land for a measly fifty cents a day. In the evenings, my grandmother Clemente had to wait for him to bring in a half of kilo of corn so that she could grind it in a metate and make tortillas for supper. There were many times that my father and his four brothers went to bed without any supper.

Grandfather Narciso died of pneumonia when the children were very young. When he died, he owed the Sotos about three hundred pesos in the hacienda store. Right after the funeral my grandmother was called to the Soto residence to discuss the money owed by the deceased. She took my father, Victor, with her, dressed in the white pants of the peon. Mr. Soto was sitting behind his desk, and leaning against the desk was a shotgun. My grandmother was offered a chair, and then Mr. Soto asked her how she expected to pay the money owed to him. She had no idea how she was going to do it, and she said so. He demanded to be paid soon. He told her if he she didn't pay, he would take her three older sons and put them to work until the debt was paid. Can you imagine, at fifty centavos a day, how long it would take to pay three hundred pesos? My grandmother started crying, and Mr. Soto got so mad and pounded so hard that the shotgun started to fall. He grabbed it to keep it from hitting the floor, and my father got very frightened. He took off as fast as he could to the little town of Imurís, which was a short distance away. He came into the pueblo shouting, "Mr. Soto is going to shoot my mother!" Naturally all the people in the village were aroused, and they were gathering together to go and save my grandmother when she arrived and cleared up everything!

That night my grandmother set about to thinking and talking things over with the children. The family decided to flee in the night so that the Sotos could not see them and stop them. The oldest son, Julián, had a two-year-old roan mare, and it was decided that he was to cross first into the United States and find work in a place that he could bring the family. He found employment right away. At that time people could come into the United States freely. My uncle Julián then returned to Mexico, and the family made preparations to leave. They packed their belongings—pots and pans and bedding and a cage with their chickens—on their burros. They prayed that on this new land a better life would open up to them, a free life where they would not work like slaves.

They crossed the border at Nogales and went east until they reached the San Pedro River, which they followed all the way north to Redington, where my uncle had a job. In those times you were able to settle down almost anywhere and build a shack and start farming. The year was 1884, and Redington had very few homesteaders. The land was fertile; there was plenty of water for farming. My grandmother and her family settled on a little corner of land close to the river. They grew corn, squash, and beans. They collected honey from beehives. They were happy because they had all the food they wanted. The boys grazed their milk goats across the river on a hill. While he was tending his goats, my father taught himself how to read!

They lived in a little hut—a jacal made of ocotillo plastered with mud inside and out to keep the cold and wind from blowing through. They lived very simply—they didn't even have kerosene lamps! They'd cut green ocotillo branches and strip the leaves and dip the tip of the ocotillo in goat tallow. When it was cold, they had to keep a fire going throughout the night in order to start a fire in the morning because matches were unheard of. Their utensils were earthenware made in Mexico. They would cut the hair from goats to make pillows, and Grandmother would use a branch from a tree to beat the matted goat's hair to fluff it.

My grandmother made her sons' shirts, underwear, and pants peon style from the manta cloth she had brought from Mexico. The pants were full with strings to tie the ankles so that dirt and insects wouldn't go up their legs. The outer shirt had a high, loose collar with long, loose sleeves. My mother had to learn to make peon-style underwear for my dad because he refused to wear American-style *calzoncillos!*

Since my grandmother couldn't afford to give her children an education, she asked a neighbor who was a professor of music to teach her children. She in turn would pay him with fryers, vegetables from her garden, and cheese from her milk goats. So my dad and his two younger brothers learned to play the violin, guitar, bass violin, and flute.

My mother also told me the story of her parents, Seráfico Montijo and Juana López. My grandfather deserted the Mexican army during the Yaqui Wars. When they were fleeing, they decided to head north into the United States. They crossed the border at Sasabe; they didn't know where they were going to stop. My grandmother was pregnant with my mother, and she had to ride the donkey most of the way. They got as far as the Casa Grande ruins near Coolidge, and my mother decided she was going to be born. My grandfather looked for a little gully in the desert where they couldn't be seen. He made a little fire and blankets from their bundles of clothing. They stayed there camping in the desert for quite a few days after my mother was born, and then they moved on. I always think of them at Christmas when I see Mary and Joseph riding a donkey looking for a place for Jesus to be born!

They went through a canyon by Florence called Cañon Quemado, and they followed it and came out by Winkleman and finally settled in a town called Calvin. My grandfather was hired to build adobe houses; that was the skill he had. They had to be built with double walls and very narrow windows because of the Apache Indians. I went there in 1923, and some of the houses that he built were still standing. They lived in Calvin for several more years and had more family, and then they decided to move to Tempe so their children could go to school. My mother grew up in Tempe; she attended a convent school there until the second grade.

My mother met my father when he was playing for a wedding in Winkleman. When they were first married, they lived in Congress, a little mining town where my father worked as a woodcutter. Later they lived for a time at the Mojaqui Mine, where Mammoth is now. Then they moved to an army post near Oracle called the American Flag, where my father panned for gold. He barely made enough to support the family. My older brothers and sisters—Rita, Carlos, Francisco, Sofía, and Cresencio—were born during this time. I was the youngest and the only child born at the Sosa Ranch on the San Pedro River.

After my parents had lived in Oracle for several years, they moved to the Sosa Ranch. My father had been looking for a place to farm because that was his weakness. He worked for Carlos Sosa for three or four years. They had acres and acres of land, and my father farmed barley, alfalfa, corn, wheat, and beans. We lived in the old Sosa ranch house that had been abandoned, and that is where I was born in 1912.

When I was about three or four years old, my parents left the Sosa Ranch and moved to Redington, where my father homesteaded a little place where he could farm and raise a few milk cows. When he was building our house in Redington, he leveled a hill down to the point where the back of the leveled hill could serve as a wall. The roof was level with the top of the hill so we could go up to the roof at any time. We used to sleep there in the summertime! It took a lot of men and mules to drag in the heavy roof beams! They laid saguaro ribs on the beams and covered them with a layer of straw and finally a mixture of straw and mud.

My father wanted to plant everything under the sun, and he did. He raised alfalfa, corn, wheat, barley, lentils, peanuts, peas, yams, and garbanzos. He planted tobacco. He made drying racks for the tobacco by laying mesh on racks made from barbed wire fencing. He didn't sell much tobacco; he gave most of it away! When he ran out of cigarette paper, Mother used to soak the tips of corn husks in water for him to use!

Isabel Montijo Vásquez
and Victor Escalante Vásquez
(ca. 1894).

We children worked with our father in the milpa. We transplanted chile and onions. We planted corn and potatoes. I used to walk on my knees on the rows my father made because we had to set the potatoes just right with the sprout side up. We carried the sprouts in a big gunny sack tied to our shoulders. And I used to cry from pain in my back from being bent over. We had to plant the corn kernels and beans in a row, and we had to measure the holes–three or four seeds in each hole, fifteen inches apart.

When father threshed the beans, he'd tie the horses to a pole, and they would go round and round. He'd remove the horseshoes so they would not break the beans, and he'd remove the horses every hour so that they would not soil the beans. The beans would settle under the plant parts, and at night if there was a little breeze they would be winnowed. Then we had to gather the beans into a can. It was hard work! No wonder I can't use my knees anymore! They're all full of arthritis.

When I was growing up, I wish I had toys, but I didn't. I used to get the biggest carrot I could find and pretend that it was my doll. I would leave the greens on top and pretend it was the doll's hair. When my mother had time, she would get some stockings and draw on eyes and a mouth and crooked little arms and floppy little feet, and that was my doll! I was twelve years old when my brother Cresencio surprised me. He had gotten a job, and he presented me with two real dolls with eyes that opened and closed. I was so happy with those dolls! But by that time I was too grown up and just kept them as keepsakes. I still have one of those dolls that he gave me. It has no eyes and no hair–just a little body!

We also raised hogs. My father had two huge wagons and three teams of horses, and he'd load the hogs on the wagons and take them to Benson to sell. It took two days! My brother Chris and I would stay with the pigs during the trip and keep pouring water over them because pigs are very delicate–they get hot and quickly die. In Benson Father would buy fabric for dresses, shoes and stockings, and other necessities. Mother didn't go because she had to stay and take care of the stock, but she was always happy with what he chose.

My father was also a blacksmith. People used to bring him the wagon wheels to repair. He also built his threshing machine and other machinery that he used

Victor Vásquez with shrine of San Isidro, patron saint of farmers, in El Rancho de los Sosa, San Pedro River Valley (ca. 1930).

on the farm. My brother Chris and I helped him in his blacksmith shop. We carried the hot iron back and forth to the water trough to cool while Father forged the hot metal at the anvil. Father was also a carpenter; he made us our furniture out of cottonwood branches.

The Mexican people who lived on the San Pedro River in those days celebrated the Feast of San Isidro, the patron saint of farmers, on the fifteenth of May. My father had a statue of San Isidro and his oxen. He built a little shrine for him and decorated it with lace and muslin linen. He fixed up a whole room in the old Sosa ranch house just for the *bulto* [statue] of San Isidro! The farmers would carry the statue from field to field and ranch to ranch. I still have a picture of my father and San Isidro in his *nicho,* and I also have the two oxen that belonged to the statue. But when my sister left the Catholic religion, she burned the saint!

There were also a lot of Mexican women in the San Pedro River Valley who had a vigil for the Holy Cross—la Santa Cruz—on May 5. They wove the branches of the elderberry tree and decorated it with flowers and herbs. They adored the cross because it represented where Jesus was nailed. A woman would say, *"Yo soy el ama de esta casa. He hablado contigo y estas de acuerdo que me vas a ayudar a subir la cruz"* [I am the head of this house. I have spoken to you, and you have agreed that you will help me raise the cross]. *"Entonces eres mi comadre de la cruz"* [That makes you my godmother of the cross]. They would have a vigil and then put the cross by the door of the house to bless the house and everyone in it.

My father was very religious, so I was very surprised when later in his life he wrote me a letter that said, "My dear daughter: We have changed religions because I have been mistaken throughout my life. One should not adore objects made by men. There is only one God, and it is only to that one God that we should kneel." And that is when he stopped playing music and gave away his guitar and his bass violin to the Iglesia Apostólica de Cristo.

My dad had a very rough life—he worked long, hard hours all of his life because he was a farmer. I can't remember him being idle or saying that he was tired. My mother used to tell him, *"Descanse,* Victor" And he would say, *"No puedo"* ["I can't rest"]. He was born into a poor family, and he was brought up to face life with a smile and to accept the hardships of life. He meant the world to me, and I think I was his pet because I was the youngest. He used to wake me up in the mornings by playing the guitar and singing "Las Mañanitas" to me. Some mornings he would stand outside by my bedroom window, and he would raise his hands and pray when the sun was coming up: *"Ana, Joaquín y María, por mis angustias postreras, hoy te invoco en este día, no me olvides, pues de veras"* ["Ana, Joaquín, and María, for my past mistakes, I ask you on this day, do not abandon me"]!

My father was also a musician. He played the violin, the bass violin, the guitar, and the flute. He could play almost every instrument except the piano, and I'm sure he could have played it if he had had one! He taught all of us to play different instruments. He taught me how to play the guitar. He traveled a lot when he was a musician. He went to all the ranches to play for the different fiestas–baptisms, weddings, and saints' days. He went to Benson, Winkleman, Mammoth, and Globe. It took three days to get to Globe! When I was about thirteen years old, I began going to the dances with him just to listen to the music. He didn't allow me to dance, but I used to dance behind the musicians where he couldn't see me! I love music because I was raised among people playing music and singing all the time, but I'm still not used to playing the radio because we never had one! Music gladdens my heart, and even now I twirl around holding my cane to show my joy when I listen to it!

My father used to repair his violin with horse hair. His violin was already old when he started out as a musician. He'd saw wood and use the fine sawdust to patch the holes. He made his own glue from the hooves of cows. He boiled the hoof until it was dry and put the marrow in a little jar. When he needed glue, he put the jar in boiling water to soften the marrow. He'd put sawdust in the crack of the instrument, add glue, and then sprinkle in more sawdust, using my mother's hairpin to push the dust into the hole.

My mother and I were also very close. She was very reserved–she never told me about the facts of life, but she did tell me about Laura Gámez, the *partera* [midwife]. Mother told me about the time she helped the midwife with a birthing. Boil and boil and boil the water! Boil and boil and boil the knives and the spoons and the rags! The woman was dying because the baby was turned sideways. The midwife tried to straighten it, and the woman was losing a lot of blood. The midwife told the husband, "Lose the wife or lose the child." "Save my wife," he said. The partera then took one of those big razors with a strap that they used in those days and cut off the baby's arm. He was delivered dead, but the mother was saved. She took a lot of time to recuperate. In those days they used olive oil on the belly button to keep the cord soft. The new mothers would stay in bed for forty days and ate only toasted tortillas, *atole* [corn-flour gruel], and roast chicken and chicken soup that were made from fryers less than three months old.

The partera used to treat *la mollera,* the soft spot on a baby's head, in this manner: she would tap the mollera with her thumb, hold the baby by the feet, and dip its head in a pan of water three times. And the soft spot would rise. The partera would also put breast milk on the mollera until it dried and then pull the fine hair on the baby's head. If a baby was left with the soft spot on its head, its eyes would dry up; it would lose its appetite and die!

There was a *curandera* in the San Pedro River Valley named Carmen Sapién. We called her "herb lady." She carried her herbs in a little bag made out of flour sacks. She would grind nutmeg into a powder and mix it with olive oil as a salve for people whose faces would get twisted from going out into the cold or if they had twitches on their mouth and eyes caused by going out in the cold when they had a fever. She made tea from the flowers of the elderberry tree for fever. For menstrual cramps she used the leaves of the *hediondilla* [greasewood] or ocotillo. She made a poultice from cottonwood leaves for a wound.

Mother made a powerful laxative from the inside part of the mesquite bark. She pounded the shavings and then put them in a quart of water with a lot of salt. She told me about a remedy that her mother made for her. She fell and broke her collarbone, and her mother cut prickly pear pads and skinned them and tied the pads on the break with splints. *Hierba del pasmo* [scarlet bouvardia] was used to doctor cattle and horses whether it was a cut or a broken leg. It was used for people, too. My father could also cure *empacho* [colic, indigestion]. I learned it from him. It is a gift from the Lord; you have to have the touch in your hands. I massage the stomach and then the spine, then pull the back. It snaps, and the obstruction leaves. When we had tonsillitis, Father would use the ham from his smokehouse. He'd rub our throat with salt mixed with pork lard and then tie a piece of ham with a rag on our throat!

We lived on our homestead, El Moral, from 1915 until 1924. My father lost the homestead even though it was in my sister's name because he was not a citizen of the United States. Charlie Bayless, who owned the Carlink Ranch, was a lawyer and tried to help my father, but he lost the homestead anyway. Two years later, in 1926, there was a big flood on the San Pedro River; the river overflowed and swept away a lot of the ranches. We could see the livestock rolling in the water. A lot of my father's friends died in that flood. They were found ten miles away buried in the river sand!

I was always very interested in learning. When we lived at El Moral in Redington, I went to the one-room schoolhouse there. The teacher would hang a book on the blackboard with the ABCs. We read about the Little Red Hen and Chicken Little. When we moved back to the Sosa Ranch after we lost the homestead, I went to school on the ranch until the eighth grade, but I never graduated. It was a little frame building between the Sosa and Vigíl house. Carlos Sosa was the superintendent. Our teacher, Mrs. Wallace, was very old and used to go to sleep during class! Mrs. Hanson was another spinster teacher; she taught me a lot. I loved geography and history; I was traveling and living in those places that I was reading about! It was hard to get young teachers—it was too isolated. Don't believe those Western movies where you see beautiful young women teaching in faraway places! It's not true!

The second time we moved back to the Sosa Ranch is when I got to know Saturnino Holguín. He was already very old. He lost his hand when fireworks

Redington School, San Pedro River Valley. Cresencio Vásquez *(front, left)* and Elena Vásquez (Cruz) *(front, third from left)* (ca. 1920).

exploded in it. They took him to Douglas, where they cauterized the wound, and later the men in the river valley made him a "hand" out of the horn of a bull! They scraped and cleaned the horn real well and attached it to the stump with leather thongs! Saturnino lived in a jacal down by the river. We children would gather around his campfire, and he would tell us stories about enchanted princesses and princes and witches and castles. Like the thousand and one nights! We never knew where he learned those stories. Maybe he just had a good imagination and made them up! He told me that he had been abducted from his cradle by Indians and taken to California. When he was about sixteen, he ran away and came to Tucson. He never knew what his real name was or who his parents were. He chose the name Saturnino Holguín because he liked the way it sounded!

Saturnino was called *"el mielero"* because he used to gather honey from hives and sell it to the people living along the river. He also lived by trapping. He trapped gray and red foxes, raccoons, and coyotes and dried the skins on a stick shaped like a Y. He sent the skins by mail to J. C. Penny's in Chicago and was paid as much as fifty cents a skin depending on the condition.

We hardly ate meat; we were practically vegetarians! We ate a lot of corn on the cob. Mother cooked *chicos* [dried tender corn kernels] and green beans with onions and red chile. She ground peas and made pea soup. She cooked navy beans with pig's feet. She made *nixtamal*. She cleaned the corn with lime and ground it to make corn meal *masa* for enchiladas and tamales. Some of the corn she ground for corn bread. Some corn she would leave whole for hominy. We made tortillas from the wheat we ground ourselves at the big old stone *molino* [mill] on the Sosa Ranch. We always had fifty or sixty *sartas* [strings] of chile, and she used it to make *carne adobada*. We'd clean the chiles with a damp cloth, remove the stems, roast the chiles in the oven, and then grind them. Mother would make a sauce with a little bit of vinegar, cover the meat, and then let it marinate for fifteen or twenty minutes on each side. Nowadays we go to the store, buy whatever it is we want, push a button, and it's done. Isn't that amazing! At Christmas time Father would fatten a couple of pigs and render the fat to make lard. We ate the *chicharrones* [cracklings]. Oh, it was so good! And Mother made pickled feet with vinegar. She

Saturnino Holguín, "el mielero," trapper and farmer (ca. 1930). His right hand prosthesis is made from the horn of a bull.

used pigs' feet to make *menudo* [a soup made with tripe, chile, and hominy] because we didn't have the real *panzas* [stomach] from the beef!

Mother had to draw water from the well to do the washing. She had a big black pot and would boil the water outside. She made bleach by letting ashes settle in a bucket of water. Rosaura Sosa taught her how to make soap out of lard. Mother would stir the water with a long stick. At night we'd fill tubs with sprinkled clothes and then iron with one of those irons that is heated on a stove. Mother washed for Carlos and Herminia Sosa, and she mended their clothes. My mother knew that I needed a few extra things as I was growing up, and that is why she took in washing and mending.

This is the story of how my brother Carlos met and married his wife, Estela Sosa Vigíl. It was the end of the school term, and my father and my brothers and sisters were going to play for the dance. The Sosas and the Gámezes all had pretty dresses, and all I had was a blue cotton dress with white trim, and I said, "But Mother, it's cotton, and the rest of the girls are wearing taffeta and silk! I'd better not go. I would feel myself so humble in just a cotton dress among the other girls!" So Mrs. Herminia Sosa—she was plump with big bosoms—brought me one of her dresses to wear. It was a beautiful white satin dress, and she had to pin it with straight pins so that it would fit me! When I was dancing, the straight pins started to poke me, so I went home and changed into my simple blue dress again!

My brother Carlos came on horseback from the Galiuro Mountains to come to the dance. My father struck up the band, and Carlos asked Estela to dance, and in those two hours they fell in love. They made an arrangement that they would write notes to each other, and I helped them by putting the notes in a can and burying it. This went on for a while until Estela's mother, Rosaura, caught me digging and found the note. Estela grabbed the note and chewed it and swallowed it! So they made another plan to signal each other with handkerchiefs—they used different colors for different messages. The red handkerchief meant "I love you." A white handkerchief meant "Everything is OK." A black handkerchief meant "We meet at midnight."

They began to make plans to marry, and my brother asked our dad to go to the Vigíls' and ask for Estela's hand in marriage. Mr. Vigíl was for it because he was my father's *compadre de la Santa Cruz*. But Mrs. Vigíl, who was a Sosa, refused. She said, "I have better plans for her." She didn't want her daughter marrying below her. You see, we were just peons. My father didn't think it was a good idea, either, but he went along. He did not think my brother would be able to provide for her in the way to which she was accustomed. Six months later Carlos went again and was again refused, so he got mad. He said, "If they won't give her to me, I'll take her. I'll find a way." So they made plans to elope, and little by little Estela hoarded clothes and hid them in the bushes.

Her mother didn't trust her, so she would lock her in her room at night. Her younger sister, Chonita, took the key from under her mother's pillow, and my brother cut a hole in the pantry screen with a wire cutter. That's how Estella escaped. My sister Rita and her husband, Alejandro Trujillo, were waiting for them in a car, and they went to Globe to get married. Mrs. Vigíl called the sheriff so he would find my brother and put him in prison, but when he found out that my brother was twenty-nine years old and Estella was twenty-one, he said, "Oh, lady, forget it!" And I got into trouble with Mrs. Sosa for being a go-between!

In time the Sosas leased their ranch to a young man from New York who was very rich. He died tragically in a plane crash while flying out to the ranch on his honeymoon. My father got a homestead in my brother Cresencio's name in the Galiuro Mountains. He raised hay and alfalfa for his cattle on a small farm in Pomerene, but it didn't pan out because he got sick. He worked for the Aguirres in Red Rock for a while and finally got another job farming for the Wilson family at the Rancho Solano near Oracle. They hired him because they had heard what a good farmer he was. He raised hogs and chickens and grew vegetables for the guests at Rancho Linda Vista, a guest ranch that the Wilsons also owned. I moved out there with my parents. It was the early 1940s, and by that time I was divorced and a single mother with two children, Gilbert Mungaray and Olga. I worked at the guest ranch also, cleaning cabins to support my children so that they could stay in school. That's when I met my husband, Rafael Cruz. He was working the cattle at the guest ranch, and when he died in 1995, we had been married for fifty-four years.

Victor Escalante Vásquez raising vegetables for Linda Vista Guest Ranch at Rancho Solano, near where the Biosphere 2 complex is currently situated (ca. 1940).

Rafael retired in 1964, but I continued working because Social Security didn't begin until 1947, and his retirement wasn't enough for us to live on. We had adopted a daughter, Edelia, and Rafael helped me raise her while I worked. He also helped me raise my daughter's oldest son. He did everything; he changed diapers, cleaned house, washed, and cooked. He even made the big Sonoran-style tortillas! We lived in Catalina, and I worked cleaning cabins at the Rail N guest ranch, which was later called the Brave Bull. Not too long ago we went there to see the old place where we lived, but it is now the Miraval Spa for rich people. It is gated, and we couldn't get in! I also worked as a maid at the Ghost Ranch Lodge, at Tucson General Hospital, and then at a nursing home. Then I worked at a company called Dumont, where they manufactured boats and airplanes that flew by remote control. I changed jobs a lot because I was always trying to earn higher wages. I worked in the laundry room at the Westward Look Resort before I retired. We washed the linens for the motel rooms and the dining rooms—hundreds and hundreds of napkins and tablecloths for the dinners and fancy banquets, and sheets and towels for the guests. We were not allowed to use the parking lot close to the hotel, and I suffered lots of pain in my legs from walking uphill from the lower parking lot to the laundry room.

I finally retired in 1983 at the age of seventy-one. We lived in a trailer in Arivaca for eleven years on property that belongs to my son, Gilbert. We moved back to Tucson for health reasons and rented a small house down the street from my daughter.

After Rafael passed away in 1995, I went to live with my daughter, Olga Donovan, who is also a widow. I still love to crochet and do needlework. My mother taught me when I was a girl. Even though we were very humble, she would try to make things beautiful. She made hooked rugs and quilted. She crocheted lace trim for our slips and camisoles and pillowcases.

Sometimes I give lessons. I give what I make as gifts to friends and family. I thank God for the blessings of my children, Olga and Gilbert. They take care of me in my old age because after all those years of working so hard I didn't have anything.

Elena Vásquez Cruz alone in her bedroom with her memories. A newspaper story about her late husband is on the wall. Photo by José Galvez (2000).

In 1994, not long after the publication of my book *Songs My Mother Sang to Me: An Oral History of Mexican American Women,* I was interviewed on the Spanish-language television program *Ayer, Hoy, y Mañana* (KUAT, Tucson) hosted by Leyla Cattan. A man was waiting in the wings for his wife, the poet Josefina Mungaray, who was also being interviewed. "You should have interviewed my mother for your book," Gilbert Mungaray told me after my interview. "She was born and raised on the Sosa Ranch on the San Pedro River and then lived for many years in the Oracle area after marrying a cowboy, Rafael Cruz. She has a lot of wonderful stories, and her memory is very vivid." Soon after that I met Elena and Rafael Cruz and began what was to become a series of interviews. Our friendship has grown over the years; I visit her and her daughter often, and she continues to share her rich and inspiring life with me.

Five generations of family
members at Elena Vásquez
Cruz's ninetieth birthday.
Photo by José Galvez (2002).

Rafael Cruz *(second from right)* with cowboy Mike Muñoz *(far right)* and Elena Vásquez Cruz's son Gilbert Mungaray *(far left)* at a line camp on Mt. Lemmon in the Santa Catalina Mountains north of Tucson (ca. 1940).

Rafael Orozco Cruz *as Told by Elena Vásquez Cruz*

Rafael asked me to marry him in the old-fashioned way—by asking my father for my hand. My father told me, "He is a good man. I think you should marry him." Rafael had already had two failed marriages and six children. I used to ask him why he drank so much, and he would tell me that he wanted to erase all the bad memories from his mind. But after we were married, he did not drink as much. He first saw that there was food in the house, and if he had five dollars left he would buy himself a pint of whiskey and drink it at home. I used to tell him he deserved it because he worked so hard bringing those wild cattle down!

My husband, Rafael Orozco Cruz, was born in a one-room adobe located between Tubac and Amado, Arizona, on April 5, 1900. His father, Manuel Cruz, ran away from home in Mexico because of his own abusive father. In fact, many years later Rafael found out that his real surname was Velásquez. His father, Manuel, had changed his name so he could not be found.

Manuel Cruz worked for different ranches in the area—Arivaca, La Tésota, and La Sierrita, where they have the mines now. He worked all the way across the Rincon Mountains from Tres Alamos to the Rancho Grande in Nogales. He worked for three different ranches belonging to the Amado family. There was no fencing in those days, and the cowboys had to travel hundreds of miles with the cattle. Rafael told me that he remembered rounding up cattle all the way from Benson to La Sierrita Mountains!

Rafael began working as a cowboy with his father at the age of seven; he learned everything about being a cowboy from his dad. They ate tortillas and *carne seca* [dried meat] for lunch and drank their water from the streams. Their days were long—from four in the morning to eight o'clock at night. Sometimes they would be gone for weeks at a time rounding up strays. Until he was eighteen years old,

Brand of Rafael Cruz

Elena Vásquez Cruz and
Rafael Orozco Cruz (ca. 1950).

Rafael and his father worked together. They earned forty-five dollars a month—
there was no extra for the boy.

Rafael didn't have much of a childhood, but he told me a very funny story about
when he was growing up. Remember I told you that my parents never told us
about the facts of life. My mother told us not to get intimate with men, that things
could happen if you got too close, but they didn't tell us what or how sexually.
But in those days if you were not a virgin on your wedding night, watch out! You
were brought back to your parents! That's what happened to a girl who lived
in Redington. The second day after the wedding the husband appeared at her
parents' home and knocked on the door and said, "Here's your daughter. I'm
bringing her back exactly the way you handed her to me!" My husband, Rafael,
was brought up in the same way. When he was a boy, there was a big dance in

Tubac for San Juan's Day. The women still wore those old-style long dresses with hoops. He and his brother were playing hide-and-seek behind the wall where the dance was being held, and they came upon a couple that was having sex. I guess they were making noises, and Rafael told his brother, "Let's go tell the people! She's killing him!" His brother had to hold Rafael back. He was older, and he knew what was going on!

One day Rafael's father was guarding some cattle that were penned up, and the gate happened to open, and there was a stampede; his father fell and broke his arm. So Rafael had to quit school and take his dad's place. Later, when his father got well, he told Rafael that he could go back to school, but Rafael never did. Rafael had only about a year of schooling, but his boss, Boyd Wilson, used to say, "He can count cattle better than I can, and I went to the university!"

In 1918 during the First World War people were dying from the Spanish flu. All of Rafael's family were sick. His mother, Leonor, died, and then fifteen minutes later his father died. Rafael told me that he went to get water for his baby brother Paulino, who was in a cradle that hung from the ceiling, and when he went to lift up his head to give him a drink, the baby was already dead. Then his sister Francisca became delirious and began hallucinating and died also. He lost his parents and a brother and a sister in one day!

The five children that survived moved to a small town named Calvin, which is by Florence, where the oldest sister, who was already married, was living. They worked the farms, irrigating barley and alfalfa. Rafael figured out that that was not the kind of work he wanted to do, but he stayed because he wanted to help support his family. When the girls were old enough to work at the dairy farms, he decided to leave–he was already twenty-one years old. He had a little mare–a roan–and one afternoon he took off and didn't go back.

He went to a ranch on the way to Florence, called El Coyote and owned by a Mr. Brady. At another ranch near Florence he met and married his first wife, Ramona. They moved to the 3C Ranch near Oracle and eventually had three children. The 3C was also owned by Mr. Brady. Rafael worked taming and breaking horses. He also helped make the adobes while the Bradys were building their house. I don't know how in the world he lived so long doing that kind of work!

Breaking horses leaves you all messed up. You don't even know if your bones are in place or not!

Rafael worked at the Rancho Linda Vista for thirty-four years, which was owned by George Wilson, a millionaire from New York. At first he hired Rafael to round up feral cattle that were scattered all over Mt. Lemmon in the Catalina Mountains. But there was a bad drought, and the Wilsons turned their cattle ranch into a guest ranch. Rafael had to break horses for the dudes, but he spent as little time with the dudes as possible! The cowboys worked day and night taming the horses so that they would be gentle enough to ride. Besides that, he used to work the cattle that belonged to Boyd and Ralph Wilson. The son and later the grandson took over the Falcon Valley Ranch after George Wilson died.

The ranch was huge! It was seventy-five square miles, halfway to Florence and Oracle, and halfway coming toward Tucson in the Tortolita Mountains. It took a whole month to finish branding and shipping! In those days cowboys had to ride miles and miles to gather up the cattle from all the different ranches in the area. Sometimes there were as many as fifteen cowboys from different ranches. Almost all of them were Mexican. The hours were long—from before the sun came up until long after the sun went down. Rafael had three horses, and he never trailered them. He had one horse for riding, one to carry his provisions, and another for extra. He'd go up into the Catalina Mountains on horseback—all the way up to where the ski lodge is now! And besides working and gathering the cattle, they branded and castrated them, earmarked the calves, dehorned and doctored them, and gave them shots! There were a lot of stray cattle that Rafael could have raised for our own, but George Wilson wouldn't let him. He said that it would not look right if the *peones* [hired help] were to raise cattle alongside the *patrón!* Later, while we were working at the American Flag Ranch in Oracle, a young vaquero gave me his mare because he had joined the army. Rafael broke her for me. Her name was Steel Dust, and when we went back to the Falcon Valley Ranch and worked for Boyd Wilson, he loaned his stud, and we raised a few horses. Our brand was the Rocking R.

Rafael worked so hard that his hands would seize up with rheumatism, and he couldn't open them! One time he caught a wild horse on the mountain and saddled

Rafael Cruz *(left)*, a well-known vaquero in southern Arizona: roundup at the Linda Vista Guest Ranch in Oracle, Arizona (ca. 1930).

him to break him, and the horse bucked so hard coming down the mountains that the sparks were flying. Blood was coming out of Rafael's ears! Another time he got caught in the rigging when a horse dumped him in a wash in the Santa Catalina Mountains. The horse went around in a circle for ten minutes before Rafael got free. Then the horse ran back to the Linda Vista, and some of the other cowboys found Rafael in the wash with one eye closed and the other bulging out of its socket and one ear nearly ripped off of his head! They got a doctor and clamped him up, but he wouldn't go to the hospital. Cowboys are like that! I finally said, "That's it. If you want to stay married to me, you have to leave the horses!"

After we were married, I continued working cleaning the guest cabins at the Rancho Linda Vista to make a little extra money so that my kids could stay in school. Rafael was making only eighty-five dollars a month. I used to earn ninety dollars a month cleaning the cabins at the guest ranch. Even my son, Gilbert, used to work lighting the fireplaces in the cabins for the guests so that he could earn a little money on tips! They gave us a little shack to live in up the wash about a mile. It had just a little kerosene heater. I had to haul rainwater out of fifty-gallon barrels to do our laundry. We bathed in a tin tub with water that I heated on the stove.

We moved from ranch to ranch for a while, trying to get better living conditions and wages. We worked at the Rail N for Mrs. Roberta Nichols. That's when I used to help with the roundups. We moved to the American Flag, back to the Linda Vista for a time, and then to the 3C and worked for Mary West, who also owned the American Flag.

It wasn't until Rafael started working for Boyd Wilson at the Falcon Valley Ranch in 1951 that we were a little better off. Rafael became the foreman because Boyd felt that he was the only one he could trust. He gave us a good house with gas and electricity and good wages–$350.00 a month. We had all the chickens and fresh eggs that we could eat and a milk cow. It is the only time in my life that I had all the beef I wanted to eat–they gave us four beeves a year, and Rafael always picked the best ones! We would make bags and bags of carne seca!

Elena Vásquez Cruz at Rancho
Solano (owned by the Wilson
family), on land near where the
Biosphere 2 complex is
currently situated (ca. 1940).

For a time while we were at the Falcon Ranch, I also worked delivering food to the cowboys. I used to drive a big four-wheel-drive truck! I'd take a big barrel of water, pots of beans, and burritos of carne seca and frijoles to feed the cowboys. Then I'd come home, wash the pots and pans and dishes, and start all over making dinner for them!

Boyd Wilson used to say of Rafael, "When they made him a cowboy, they broke the mold. They don't make them like that anymore." Rafael even made his own *reatas* [lassos] and *cabestros* [halter ropes]. To make the cabestros he made two wooden shuttles with little holes shaped like an arrowhead. It takes two people to make the cabestros. One person would turn the little sticks around and around, and Rafael would keep adding horse hair until it was the right length, like a spinning wheel. He used two sticks shaped like an arrow with a hole in the middle to twist the hair. When the strands of hair were the right length, Rafael would braid them. When he made the reatas, he would soak the cowhides for three or four days and then cut the hide into strips. He then would tie a gadget to a mesquite tree and put two blades on two lengths of boards and pull the strips of leather slowly until they were the length he wanted. Then he would soak them again, and the next day he would braid six strands of hide into reatas.

Rafael retired at the age of sixty-six after almost sixty years of living the hard life of a cowboy. In February 1995, just before he died, Bonnie Henry, a columnist for the *Arizona Daily Star,* wrote an article about Rafael called "Vanishing Vaquero." She wrote that "Rafael was an icon of the American West, sporting chaps and spurs and a gaze level and true. No wonder every little boy wants to be one. No wonder few men are."

Josefina Mungaray, who is my son's wife, wrote a beautiful poem called "Añoranzas del Vaquero Rafael Cruz" [The laments of the cowboy Rafael Cruz] in Rafael's honor. I read it at his funeral.

Le tuve amor al rancho
Desde mi temprana edad
Fue mi delicia el caballo
Cuando ya pude montar.

Me crié entre las lomas y cerros
Fui víctima de orfandad
Pero de ser un vaquero
Nadie me lo pudo quitar.

La primera vez que ensillé
Me sentí muy orgulloso
Porque entonces me pasié
En un caballo barroso.

Que a veces se asustaba
Hasta con su misma sombra
Derechito se paraba
Cuando se movía una hoja.

Comencé a trabajar
Primero de caporal
Y me gustaba lazar
Mansos y broncos igual.

El dueño del dicho rancho
No hablaba español
Era de sangre tejano
Pero también buen patrón.

Cuando ascendí a mayordomo
Fue para mí una sorpresa
Empecé a creer que aquí
Ponía fin a mi pobreza.

Conozco como a mis manos
La Catalina y Limón
Porque por algunos años
Saqué el ganado orejón.

El Puerto del Charaló
Es sin duda fiel testigo
Que el eco de mi voz
Aun es fuerte y vivo
De cuando arriaba yo
El ganado con mis gritos.

Y si alguna se desviaba
O se quedaba perdida
Mi hijo Ramón me ayudaba
Y antes de morir el día
En nuestras manos estaba.

Me acostumbré a vivir
En el rancho y ser leal
A mi patrón y así
Ganarle la voluntad.

Los años fueron pasando
Pero yo no los sentía
Porque había hecho del rancho
Mi más alegre familia.

Un día menos pensando
Tuve que decirle adiós
Al que entregué los años
Mi salud y mi devoción.

Por las noches cuando duermo
Me sueño en aquel rancho
Donde trozaba los cuernos
Alegre y entusiasmado
A los pequeños becerros.

Y de la cama yo salto
Porque oigo bramar

Las vacas de dicho rancho
Donde yo pude dejar
Gigantes gotas de llantos.

Mi vida al paso lento
Va llegando al final
De lo que es mi camino
Y yo doy gracias al cielo
Que me dejó disfrutar
De lo que fue mi destino.

En las cuestiones de amor
Fui ciego y desdichado
Esposas que tuve yo
Por otros me abandonaron.

Pero hubo otra en mi vida.
Que en el interior del ser
La traigo siempre prendida.
Y es mi Elena querida.

Y entregarle lo que yo
Había acaparado
Solo heridas y dolor
De un corazón destrozado.

Pero así me aceptó
Y ante Dios me prometió
Serme fiel y con orgullo
Ahora lo digo yo
Que es uno nuestro amor
Y lo será hasta el sepulcro.*

*Josefina Mungaray, "Añoranzas del Vaquero Rafael Cruz," used by permission of the author.

I loved the ranch life
From a very early age.
When I learned to ride,
Horses became my delight!

Because I was an orphan,
I was raised among the ridges and hills
But no one could rob me
Of my vaquero skills.

The first time that I mounted a horse
I felt so very proud!
And I went riding for miles
On that red horse!

A horse so afraid of its own shadow that
Sometimes he would stand
Stock still
If a leaf trembled!

I began to work
As a foreman.
How I loved to rope
The broncos as well as the tame ones!

The owner of the ranch
Didn't speak Spanish
He was a Texan
But a good boss!

When I became the ranch manager
It came as a big surprise
I began to think that at last
My days of poverty were over!

I know the Catalinas and Mt. Lemmon
Like the backs of my hands!
Because for a number of years
That's where I gathered wild cattle!

The place they call Charalois Gap
Is without a doubt a faithful witness
That the echo of my voice
Is still strong and alive
From the times that I rounded up
The cattle with my cries.

And if one dogie strayed
Or perhaps was lost
My son Ramón helped me.
And before the day was done
We had captured it.

I was accustomed to ranch life
And being loyal to my boss,
And in that manner
Gained his good will.

The years went passing by
But I really didn't feel them.
The ranch had become a haven
Of happiness for my family.

And then, one day without warning
I had to say good-bye
To the one I had given my life,
My health, and all of my devotion

Even now, at night when I sleep
I dream of that beloved ranch

Where with enthusiasm and joy
I wrestled with the horns
Of the little calves.

And I jump from my bed
Because I think I hear the lowing
Of the cattle from that ranch
Where I left
Gigantic tear drops.

My life is passing by slowly
And now I'm arriving at the end.
But I thank the heavens
For the journey I have made
And for the destiny
That has been mine.

In matters of love
I was blind and unlucky
The wives that I had
Abandoned me for others.

But there was another in my life
Whom I always carry
Deep within my soul
And that is my beloved Elena.

I gave to her
The only gift I had
The wounds and pain
Of a broken heart.

But she embraced me
And promised before God
To be faithful to me.

And now I declare
Our one true love
Which I will carry to my grave!

Teresa Mendivil Gradillas underneath the black walnut tree whose nuts she collected as a child at the Mendivil brothers' family ranch in Benson, Arizona. Photo by José Galvez (2002).

Teresa Mendivil Gradillas

I was born on October 8, 1926, in Benson, Arizona. My parents' names were Pedro Arcia Mendivil and Carlota Figueroa Quihuis. My father was born in 1900 on a ranch called Tres Alamos, which was about ten miles north of Benson on Ocotillo Road. My paternal grandfather, Eutimio Mendivil, was born in Chinán, Sinaloa, Mexico, in 1859. My paternal grandmother, Juana Arcia, was born on the Tres Alamos Ranch in 1876. It was a very large ranch owned at one time by the Grijalva family. My grandfather Eutimio worked for them as a cowboy, and that is where he met my grandmother Juana. The area was like a little town—it even had a school and a grocery store. My grandmother and her sister, Petra, and her brother, Francisco, all attended school in Tres Alamos. Now that big ranch has been all broken up, and people have built houses out there. The Kartchner family of Kartchner Caverns State Park now own a lot of the land where the Tres Alamos used to be. I don't think that any of those old buildings exist anymore.

My maternal grandparents names were Eulalia Figueroa and Rafael Quihuis On the Quihuis side, my great-grandfather also had a ranch in the Tres Alamos area. He also owned property and several houses in Benson. The ranch was the cause of my grandfather's death—a mule he was riding ran and threw him off, and he suffered a head injury. He eventually died of that injury. He was only fifty-five years old. He left the ranch to my aunt Rita, who was married to José Bernal, and now the land belongs to the Bernal family.

At one time my grandfather Eutimio Mendivil returned to Mexico—he had another family there—and he brought back another son, also named Eutimio. His nickname was Tío Güero. He remained with the family and was always treated as one of their own. When my grandfather died in 1922, the family moved to Benson. My father and his brothers began to work for the Apache Powder Plant, an explosives company in St. David, and at a chicken ranch in Pomerene. My father and my *tío* Claudio also worked at the Miers Grocery Store in Benson and at a meat market owned by Badelio Martínez. Times were hard, and my grandmother Juana also worked as a laundress for the Motel Arnold. Her sons helped her out there also—they did a lot of different things to survive.

In 1928 Claudio, my father's oldest brother, filed the papers for the family homestead, which was located about three miles west of Benson. The brothers and sisters—Claudio, Eutimio, Eulalia, Delfina, Emiteria, Francisca—their half-brother Tío Güero, my grandmother's brother Francisco, and my grandmother Juana all moved out to the Mendivil Brothers' Ranch. At first they lived in a temporary place, but in time they built a small adobe house, a barn, and bunkhouses for the bachelor brothers. All the sisters stayed at the ranch until they were married, but my *tía* Lala [Eulalia] never married.

The original homestead was a total of 240 acres, and they leased about three sections. Later on they bought another section down below where the big corrals are, so the ranch was fairly large with the deeded land and the leased land. It reached almost all the way to the present-day road to Sierra Vista on the east and bordered the Burt Smith Ranch on the west. Even though my uncle Claudio was the one who filed for the homestead, all the brothers had a share, and they all worked the ranch. They were very united. They each had their own brand as well as the company brand. We continued living in Benson, but even when my dad was working at the powder plant, he would go to help at the ranch when he'd come home from work. And during the depression, when jobs were scarce and times were hard, we'd pack up, and they'd come after us in a horse-drawn wagon, and we'd all go and stay over there. And that's where my memories of the ranch come from.

In the beginning, before they bought their truck, my great-uncle Francisco would come after us and take us to church in Benson in a horse-drawn wagon. I don't remember my grandmother being very religious, but she did attend mass regularly and celebrated her saint's day. All of her friends would come to the ranch on *el día de San Juan*. I especially remember one big celebration. I was small, but I'll never forget! One of my grandmother's friends taught her how to make home

Eutimio Arcia Mendivil *(left)* and Pedro Mendivil at the Mendivil Brothers' Ranch in Benson, Arizona (1928).

Carlota Quihuis Mendivil and children Teresa *(seated, front)* and Miguel at the Mendivil Ranch west of Benson, Arizona (ca. 1930).

brew. They had root beer for the children and *teswín* [a fermented corn drink] and *bizcochuelos* [anise cookies]. She put the beer and root beer in the sand in the arroyo to keep it cool. They brought a band out from Tucson and danced on the dirt patio in front of the house!

I was eight years old when my grandmother Juana died, but I remember her well. She was a very strong and hard-working woman. She knew all about ranching—she must have learned it from her parents when she was living at Tres Alamos. She rode a horse; she gathered the cattle and horses and took them to the pastures and brought them back to the corrals. She searched for the cattle on the range when they were lost; she plowed and planted their fields with mule-drawn plows. She took care of the milk cows and fed the chickens and the turkeys that they raised.

They raised crops by the rains that came—they called it *"el temporal."* They raised all kinds of vegetables for the family to use—corn, beans, chile, tomatoes, pumpkins, squash, and watermelons. We'd go out to the field, and she'd break open a watermelon, and we'd eat it right there out in the field. And—I know it's hard to believe—she'd dig a hole in the arroyo and cover the watermelons with sand, and we'd have watermelons in December! My daughters, Rita and Ana María, don't believe me when I tell them! She used to dry the squash and string beans and chile—it's called *chile pasado*. My grandmother would harvest the corn and dry it and have *nixtamal* for *menudo* [a soup with chile, tripe, and hominy]. She'd grind it and make *masa* for tortillas and tamales. We called the dried squash *"rueditas"* ["little wheels"]; she would soak them in water, and we'd have fresh squash. Oh, it was so delicious! Nowadays they have what they call dehydrating machines— well, the old dehydrating machine was a screen and a sheet!

My father and my uncles had a client in Tombstone who would buy half a beef, and whatever was left they'd come into Benson to sell. And whatever they couldn't sell they would make into jerky. My grandmother would dry the meat and kept turning it and turning it. They would buy the used feed sacks from a neighbor who was a chicken farmer. They'd wash them and put the jerky in them and store them in the barn. My grandmother was a very good cook, and she'd use that *carne seca* for tamales and *chile colorado* [red chile] and tamale pie and even make *chiles rellenos* with it! They raised their own rabbits in cages in the barn, and when they'd kill them, they'd hang them from a big old mesquite tree that is still there on the property. My grandmother had a little grinder, and she'd grind the rabbit meat and make hamburgers as well as *albóndigas* [meatballs] with it!

When I was young, they gave me a little calf, as well as one to my brothers Miguel and Roberto. And those calves kept producing! When I was going to school, I would ask about my calf to see if it was fattening up so they could sell it. They let me keep the money, and I put it in a savings account in Benson but lost it when the banks failed during the depression.

My tía Panchita [Francisca] liked to bake and cook. They used a big wood-burning stove, and I liked to watch her. There is a black walnut tree on the old homestead that's still alive, and I used to chop all the nuts from that tree when

RS

Brand of Pedro Mendivil
(Father)

she made her fudge and cookies and cakes. I learned how to bake with my aunt. And Tía Lala would make cheese—mainly quesadillas—and I remember watching my mother turning the churn to make butter.

I remember that I would see some of the kids in school during the depression, and they didn't always have enough to eat. My friends thought we were rich, but we didn't have any money. One of my friends from those days tells me, *"Tú nunca supiste hambre."* It's true—we never went hungry because the family raised everything. A lot of people went out to the ranch in those hard times, and my aunts and uncles would feed them. They were very generous.

The only things we had to worry about during the depression was our clothing. But my tía Lala would use those grain and flour sacks and make aprons and dishtowels and pinafores, and one time she even made *calzones* [underwear]! She made them for her sisters, and they didn't want to wear them! She even made me a dress once from the sacks! Tía Lala also did needlework. She taught my sister Josie how to crochet.

I don't like to go out there now and see the place because it's all tumbled down and in ruins. It used to be so green and pretty, with lots of mulberry and cottonwood trees. To me it was beautiful. A retired lieutenant colonel owns the property now where the houses and the barn are. It looks terrible—completely ruined. There's nothing there now, and all the buildings are falling down. I don't know why they don't just knock it all down and forget about it.

Not long ago I was in Mesilla, New Mexico, and I went outside to sit in the plaza while my daughter was shopping in one of the stores. There was a man and a woman playing the guitar and singing the old Mexican song about ranches called "Cuatro Milpas," and I started to cry. When my grandson saw me, he got worried and went back to get my daughter. "What's wrong, Mother?" my daughter asked. "Don't you feel well?" "It's nothing, hija. It's just when I hear that song 'Cuatro Milpas,' it reminds me of our family ranch, and it makes me sentimental."

🚍 I learned about cousins Teresa Mendivil and Tim (Eutimio) Mendivil through Peter Mendivil, a high school friend of my daughter, Elena. Peter's father,

Fernando Mendivil, put me in touch with them. On my first visit to Benson in September 2002, I spent time getting acquainted with the area and with the Mendivil family history. Tim Mendivil took me, along with Teresa, to the property adjacent to his present home, where the Mendivil Brothers' Ranch had once thrived. He also showed me some old abandoned corrals and cattle chutes below the ranch buildings and drove us along the west side of the San Pedro River toward the area of Tres Alamos, north of Benson. I returned there on October 23, 2002, to record the interviews with Teresa and Tim, and again in November to accompany José Galvez on his photo shoot.

Teresa Mendivil married Arturo Gradillas in 1949. Her husband worked at the Apache Powder Plant and passed away in 1985. She has two daughters, Ana María Meza and Rita Eissmon. She worked at various jobs during her marriage and had a clerical position for thirty years at Fort Huachuca, from which she retired in 1987. She continued to work part-time for ten years as a front desk receptionist at the Best Western Hotel in Benson, Arizona. She lives in a home that she and her husband bought in 1959, located around the corner from her childhood home in Benson.

Tim Mendivil looks in on the
condition of the old Mendivil
brothers' ranch house in
Benson, Arizona. Photo by
José Galvez (2002).

Tim (Eutimio) Mendivil

I was born in Tucson, Arizona, on September 15, 1948, and raised here on our family ranch, which is located about three miles west of the town. My father's name was Eutimio Arcia Mendivil. He was born in 1903 at the Tres Alamos Ranch, which is located about ten miles north of Benson. He died in 1993 at the age of ninety. My mother's name is Amparo Gastelum de Mendivil. She was born at Maune, Sinaloa, Mexico, in 1906. She is now ninety-six years old and lives with me and my family at our home, which I have built on part of what was the Mendivil Brothers' Ranch, which had belonged to my uncles and father.

I never met my paternal grandfather, Eutimio Mendivil, for whom I was named. He died long before I was born. But my father used to tell me stories about him. He said he was a cowboy from way back. I think that's all he did all his life, cowboyin'. He worked on a bunch of ranches all over the place. He worked for the Grijalvas at Tres Alamos. He might be buried at the old cemetery at Tres Alamos, but I think it's been bulldozed.

My paternal grandparents' names were Sixto Gastelum and Paulita Armenta. My grandfather Sixto was a jack-of-all-trades. For a time he had a barbershop down on Calle Meyer in Tucson. He also did a little trading between here and Sinaloa, and during those times he would take the family back and forth between here and Mexico. He was a cowboy also. He worked on ranches in the Tanque Verde area east of Tucson and for the Corbett family, who had a ranch west of Tucson by A Mountain.

I know that until he was about eighteen years old, my father worked full-time as a cowboy. He cowboyed with the Boquillas Cattle Company; they used to have all the land over here in the Whetstone Mountains. He told me that once their boss left them there at a line camp with no food, and all they ate were rabbits! They had some flour and made bread, but that was about it! My uncle Claudio,

Eutimio Arcia Mendivil at the
Mendivil Brothers' Ranch in
Benson, Arizona (ca. 1950).

my father's oldest brother, was an old-time cowboy, too. He cowboyed all his life; it wasn't until he was in his late forties that he started working for the Apache Powder Plant. After they had their own ranch, they couldn't make it on just the ranch alone, so they all worked for the Apache Powder Plant in St. David at one time or another.

Then, of course, they both cowboyed for the Mendivil Brothers' Ranch. The ranch was in Claudio's, the oldest brother's, name, but they all had a share—a gentlemen's agreement. My dad lived on the ranch with his mother, Juana; his sisters; his brother Claudio; a half-brother, Tío Güero; and one of his uncles, Tío Chico [Francisco]. My uncle Pedro [Pete], Teresa's father, lived with his family in town.

When my dad married my mother, he was forty-five years old. My mother had been married previously in Mexico but was widowed. They met each other through their families, who knew each other in Sinaloa. I am their only child. My dad built his own house on the ranch as soon as they were married. Tío Pete and Tío Chico helped him build the house; they made the adobes themselves. It is still standing, and I rent it to an old cowboy named Armando Bernal, who helps take care of my roping steers and horses for me.

The original homestead was 240 acres, and they had a lease of about three sections. Later on they bought another section down below where the big corrals are. I remember how the ranch looked in the early days; it was all fixed up pretty and cheerful. The ranch house had a big screened porch, and there were several outlying buildings, including a barn and bunkhouses that the bachelor brothers used for sleeping. There were corrals where they kept and fed the cattle in the bad times when it didn't rain and a barn that they used to store the hay. They would order a semi from Casa Grande—about ten or twelve tons of hay every winter. They also used the barn for butchering and hanging the beef. There was a *pila* [trough] with a windmill where they pumped water. Later on they did run out of water—the well collapsed. I remember that my dad used to come in from work and go to my uncle Pete's in Benson and haul about 250 gallons of water to the ranch every day in a big old tank that he had on the back of his truck. In the early days they also did a little farming—but when the well dried up, they stopped.

Eutimio Arcia Mendivil *(left)* and Pedro Mendivil at the Mendivil Brothers' Ranch in Benson, Arizona (ca. 1950).

They had a barbecue pit; my uncle Claudio was really good at making barbecue for all the weddings around here. He and my uncle Pete made a big hole–about six feet deep and four feet wide. They put rocks down at the bottom of the hole and lined it with mesquite wood. Then they'd season the meat with spices and wrap it in *guangoche,* gunnysacks, and put it in tubs and lower it into the hole. Then they covered it with tin and dirt and made sure that it was sealed so that no smoke could get out. They'd put it in sometime in the late afternoon–around six or seven when it was getting dark–and they'd watch it all night. They used to party all night while they were watching the meat! *Una paranda!* I helped them do it two or three times, when I was about thirteen or fourteen years old. In the morning, when the meat was ready, they'd take it out, and the meat would fall off the bones. Oh, it was so good! They used to make chorizo, too, and *morcilla*. That's when they kill the cow and drain the blood. Then they'd cook the blood with tomato and onion. Some people really think it's delicious. They'd also roast the head of the cow in the pit and make *taquitos* with freshly made tortillas. They'd use all the parts of the cow! There was always something going on at the old place!

One of my cousins sold the land where all the old ranch buildings were—to a lieutenant colonel who said he is going to fix it up. *Pero no va a hacer nada.* But he's not going to do anything. I think he just bought it for an investment. I go through there sometimes, and I can't take it; I just keep going. I used to see all the *viejitos* [elders] over there—Tío Chico *cortando leña* [cutting firewood], Tío Claudio hanging a beef, Tío Pete making *carne seca. Una de las tías haciendo tortillas en la estufa de leña* [one of the aunts making tortillas outside on a wood-burning stove]. It was always very lively—*todos los viejitos dando guerra* [all of the elders fussing around].

When they had the ranch, there was open range, and they ran about two hundred head. Plus, they had about eight or ten brood mares so that they could raise their own horses. My uncle Claudio, as I told you, was quite a cowboy; he was a bronc rider. He's the one who used to ride all the wild horses—tame them down. And my dad and Uncle Pete used to rein them—finesse them. They needed to have good horses because they rode all over the place checking their cattle—all over the Whetstones and then down the San Pedro River. Then in the late 1930s they had to cut down the herd until they got the state leases. Then they could run only about sixty head. At that time they would take the cattle to the sales in Willcox and Tucson. They'd truck them in; my dad had an old Dodge pickup with a rack on it.

My dad told me a story of a roundup they went on in the early days of the ranch. At that time the railroad was in Sierra Vista, so they took them on a cattle drive all the way to Fry; there were some stockyards there. There were about two hundred head on that cattle drive—theirs as well as some that belonged to other ranch-

Brand of Claudio Mendivil (Uncle)

ers. It took them about four or five days! Uncle Pete and Tío Chico had the chuck wagon with the food and bedrolls. It was during the depression, and they had to sell most of their cattle to make it.

My dad showed me how to ride a horse when I was about three years old. I used to ride with him way out toward the Whetstones to rope and castrate cattle. We'd ride for miles to fix fences, haul salt block, and take winter supplements— *un poquito de todo*. A little bit of everything. I'd go on roundups with him; I'd help him brand. I learned to rope with him, chasing calves out there in the sticks. I was out there ropin' when I was about ten or eleven. It was a lot of work, but a lot of fun.

My dad always really liked horses; he always had two or three really good ones—the best around. After I started ropin', I'd go with him to rodeos. He'd jackpot—compete in the local team ropin'. We did some calf ropin', too. He told me the story of how one year when he was about thirty years old, they had a calf ropin' in Redington down on the San Pedro River. There was a world champion roper out there, a *gabacho* [an Anglo]. He was supposed to be real good and all that. People bet all kinds of money. They told my dad, "This guy can beat you." And he said, "Okay. I'll try." So he went down there and beat that gabacho. The world champion! He was real proud of that! They used to have the rodeos down there in Redington at the Sosas' and at the Ronquillos'. My uncle Claudio was the best bronc rider, but my dad was the best roper! He roped until he was about eighty years old—we'd go together, and we won a few ropings together. I used to head for him; he used to heel. It comes from an old vaquero ranching tradition. One cowboy would catch the head and the other the feet so that when the calf or steer was knocked down, they could stretch him out to brand or doctor him.

When the Mendivil brothers were all working the ranch, they all had their own brand as well as the company brand. My dad's brand was R Triangle—my dad got that brand from the Quihuis family on his mother's side; there were only three of them, Ramón, his son, and his wife, and I guess that's what the triangle stood for. I still have that brand. My uncle Claudio's brand was C8. The C stands for Claudio, and there were eight in the family. RS was my uncle Pedro's brand—he

Brand of Eutimio Mendivil (Father) inherited from Quihuis side of the family (Maternal)

bought the brand from another rancher. Each brother had their own cattle, and then there were cattle that belonged to the company.

My uncle Claudio lived to be in his late nineties, and as I have said, his was the only name on the deed. He started giving some of the land away to a friend, and my dad and Uncle Pete tried to talk some sense into him, so he finally gave what was left to the brothers. My uncle Pete gave up his share, and my dad told my uncle Claudio, "Don't give it to me; I'm old. Give it to my son." So I ended up with fifty-two acres, and one of my cousins, my aunt Delfina's son, has sixty-two acres.

I graduated from Benson High School in 1966 and then went to barber school and then got drafted. I went to Vietnam, and when I got back from the service, I went to Tucson for a few years. And that's when I met my wife, Socorro Murietta, who is from Trincheras, Sonora. We were married in 1970 and have four sons—Jorge Eutimio, Jaime Alberto, Martín Eduardo, and César Antonio. After we got married, I continued barbering for about four years, and then I landed a job with the civil service in Fort Huachuca as a truck driver and then a warehouse foreman. After my dad started getting old, I moved back up to the ranch. In 1991 I built a new house on the land I inherited from my father. I put in my twenty-six years in the civil service and left. I'm retired now but go in to Tucson a few days a week to help out at my son Jaime's barbershop.

I've always liked horses, and I've always had a horse to ride. Sometimes I would get on broncs, and my dad would say, "You get off that horse! He's too wild for you!" But I'd ride him anyway! I guess you could say that I'm the one that's continuing the tradition. Once in a while I buy a horse and break him—make a little money on it. As a matter of fact, I've got two for sale right now. I bought a trail horse for twelve hundred dollars—they were afraid of him. I rode him for a few weeks and trained him, and now he's ready for ropin'. I could get five thousand dollars for him now! As a matter of fact, our son Jorge, who is a schoolteacher and football coach at San Manuel High School, used to earn extra money breaking horses while he was in school! He worked for Mr. Goodman in St. David, who raised horses, and Mr. Goodman paid him about three hundred dollars for each horse that he broke.

Tim Mendivil helps out at his son's barbershop in Tucson when he's not on his ranch in Benson, Arizona. Photo by José Galvez (2002).

Three of our sons have their own horses and rope. They all won buckles when they were little. Tony won his first buckle when he was eight years old! He has a five-acre place west of Tucson in the area of Robles Junction, where he keeps his horses. I've won four or five buckles. I keep eight or ten calves, and we have our own arena here at the house that we use for practicin' and tunin' up for the jack-pots—the local competitions. Our sons come to practice once or twice a week. We go all over the place—Tucson, Phoenix, as far as New Mexico. Jaime and I won a real big one here in Benson. Now our ten-year-old grandson, Jorge's son Eutimio, has started ropin', too. He's the fifth generation! He's about ready. As a matter of fact, this summer I'm going to take him with me to all the jackpots.

Our son Jorge will get my dad's old place—he was always real close to him and moved over to their house on the ranch when he was about eight. He lived with his grandparents there and took care of them and helped them out. He's got my dad's old saddle and his old spurs. He'll keep the ropin' goin', keep the tradition goin'.

Three generations of cattle
ropers: Tim Mendivil, his son
Jorge, and his grandson
Eutimio at the Mendivil Ranch
in Benson, Arizona. Photo by
José Galvez (2002).

Joe Quiroga unloads his horse,
Julio, as he prepares to round
up cattle on the Diamond C
Ranch outside Elgin, Arizona.
Photo by José Galvez (2002).

Joe Quiroga

I was born in Patagonia, Arizona, on March 19, 1937. My parent's names were Maclovia Nañez and Joaquín Quiroga. My mother, Maclovia, was born in one of the mining camps of Helvetia in the Santa Rita Mountains. My father, Joaquín, and two of his brothers came here from Sonora, Mexico, between the years 1915 and 1920. I suppose they came because of the opportunities to work. Things were not too great in Mexico at that time. They were not too great here either!

My father was a miner by trade, but he also did a little bit of agriculture. He used to plant wherever he could, especially during the depression, when things were real tough. He used to dry farm, mainly—any parcel of land that he could get a hold of! He farmed in the Patagonia area—all the bottom lands that were available, empty lots, that sort of thing. He planted beans, corn, squash—the kinds of vegetables that would keep. He bartered a bit, as well as raising food for the family. We also raised chickens, pigeons, and rabbits. So there were always a lot of chores to do around the house. There were so many of us that each was designated what responsibilities he had: tending or watering the livestock or watering the garden. There were a dozen of us children. Two or three besides the ones who survived had died in infancy.

I have fond memories of our father. He wasn't as much of a disciplinarian as our mother was. He was very hard working, and he always showed a lot of affection to all of us kids. Everybody felt that he or she belonged to the unit, and everybody felt secure although we had very little in the way of material goods. We were raised in very primitive habitations—houses with dirt floors—but we always felt secure, even in those settings! We lived in several places, usually rented apartments. One of them is right next to the López Pool Hall, and we also lived in the Cody Hall Complex. Father bought a place up in one of the canyons. It was an old house that we mostly used as a barn. He had planned to build a house there before he passed away. Father died in 1947; I was still quite young. My youngest brother was only one year old.

I have many memories of my mother. She was a very kind woman. She would literally take her shirt off her back to give it to you if she thought you needed it worse than she did. She was a very hard-working woman, obviously. She had twelve kids to tend to! What astounds me is that today people think that they work hard, and they don't even begin to touch the surface of what women in that era had to do. Mother used to do the laundry for our big family outside in a tub. We used to have to go miles to get wood. She would fell the trees herself with an ax, and then, after doing all of that, she would come home and make tons of food for the horde! It was a tough life for her, but she took it in stride. Nothing seemed to disturb her.

Maclovia Nañez Quiroga in
Patagonia, Arizona (ca. 1960).

You were commenting on the huge oak in this area. If there happened to be a dead one, it was nothing for her and our *tía* Chica to fell it. One of them would get on one side of the tree, and the other would get on the other side, and they'd start chopping at that thing until they felled it! Then they would quarter it. On those wood-cutting days, we used to take three or four burros with pack saddles and load them and shuttle wood while my mother and Tía Chica would continue to chop. We'd pack a lunch of bean burritos and water. We used to get a great deal of wood in one day. Today most people with a chain saw wouldn't get as much wood as our mother and aunt did with an ax! Our tía Chica was married to our father's brother, Uncle Ramón. She was an Opata Indian from down in Navajoa. She was a big and strong woman, and I have very fond memories of her as well.

Oh, how I remember my mother's cooking! She used to love to cook with garlic. My wife, Noemi, and I were already living in Elgin, and we used to go to Patagonia to go to mass and visit on Sundays with the rest of the family. And we'd turn on the street where Mother lived, and I'd know Mother was cooking because I could smell the garlic from blocks away!

As I said, Mother was the disciplinarian in the family. She was not afraid to strap us. In this day and age they don't believe that this is the thing to do, but we were never traumatized. We knew that we were being punished because we deserved it. Nowadays people believe that children are traumatized by a whack on the butt. I don't buy it, but I'm not a psychologist, so I can't say if it is right or not.

When our father died, everybody pitched in. The older brothers and sisters went to work. Mother used to bake in a big wood stove, and we used to peddle the empanadas and bread that she made. On the weekends she'd make *menudo* [a soup with chile, tripe, and hominy], and early in the morning we'd be delivering pots of menudo throughout the neighborhood. My older brother worked in the mines or at whatever jobs were available. I started working cleaning yards at a very early age. In fact, one of the places I used to clean seemed like miles out in the countryside when it was really only about a mile and a half from town. So that's how we survived—by doing what was available!

When I was in high school, I started working in the mines during summer vacations. I was seventeen years old or so. I worked there for two or three summers, so I got a lot of experience. I had the opportunity to work with different tradesmen—the pipe fitters, diamond drillers, timber men, and the actual miners—so I was exposed to a lot of different skills.

Whatever we earned went to the house. If Mother chose to give us some money, she would, and that was welcome. But we all knew that what we earned was a contribution to the whole family.

Patagonia was a nice small community when I was growing up. It was multicultural, but a little more toward the Mexican. I remember that the white friends we had spoke Spanish along with the rest of us. Most of the white people were bosses or supervisors at the mines, and they had to learn Spanish to communicate with the workers. The economy was based on the mines and also on cattle ranching, but it was mostly the mines that drove the economy. Because of the mines, the train used to come in to bring material and ship out ore. Ranchers in the area would use the railroad to ship cattle also.

Patagonia was never a very large town. At the height of the mining activity it never had more than twelve or fourteen hundred people. It was a very close-knit community. I remember that during the depression everyone was concerned about everyone else's welfare, and consequently a lot of people helped one another. It was more of a day-to-day thing. Nowadays it seems that the only time a community comes together is when there is a natural disaster.

It was a happy place for a kid to be raised in. Recreation was the easy part. Of course, we had Sonoita Creek, which was a great playground. We had swimming holes and fishing. We used to go down to the creek and spend a whole day if we could. We were allowed to roam free for a certain amount of time, but if we got carried away, we'd pay for it! Sometimes we'd take our burros for miles down the river. We'd have slingshots and used to kill lizards and birds. That was not too animal friendly! We'd have a competition, and we used to keep score. The smaller the animal, the fewer points given. Once in a while we'd score a squirrel! We'd seine the native fishes that are protected now. We used a gunnysack and then skewered them and roasted them! They were just sardine size, but you could get plenty with a gunnysack. Apparently that wasn't too harmful because although they're endangered, they're still around.

There was also a stockyard in Patagonia. We'd play tag around the top rails. It was eight feet high, but I don't recall anyone being hurt; I would consider it dangerous now. It taught us a lot of agility. Swimming and walking in the river also taught us coordination, and so our bodies developed. That is what conditioned us and prepared us for later life and the workforce, I suppose.

There were two events that the community participated in—San Juan's Day on June 24 and the Fourth of July, a couple of weeks later. Everybody would go down to Sonoita Creek and picnic all day long; it was a day in the countryside. On San Juan's Day there would be horse races. The farmers used to believe that the rainy season began on San Juan's Day, and they would welcome that because their crops would get an early start. I know that even now in the small villages in Mexico they celebrate the saint's day in anticipation of the monsoons and the rainy season. On both San Juan's Day and the Fourth of July musicians would roam from party to party and family to family. There used to be a lot of musicians in Patagonia!

I didn't know how to speak English when I started school, and consequently several teachers were hard on me. We were disciplined for speaking Spanish on the playground. We didn't know another language, so we really didn't have an alternative. Until we got a grasp of English, we had to disobey if we wanted to have any communication at all. It was hard. I love to read. I read a lot, and I suppose that is why I speak English so well now. Mother didn't learn to speak English until she was in her seventies. We'd tease her, and she would regress, but after we all left home, she could make herself understood. Father knew how to read and write English. I'm not sure what his schooling was, but I think he picked it up along the way with his work.

As soon as I finished high school, I married my high school sweetheart, Noemi Cruz, and we started a family. I had aspirations to go to college and become a history teacher, but because of economics I had to start work. There were no loans or scholarships or grants, at least not that I was aware of. Consequently, right out of high school I started working on a ranch, and I've been doing ranch work ever since!

Brand of Joe and Noemi Quiroga

Noemi Cruz Quiroga and
José Quiroga (1957).

I worked on the Babocómari Ranch right after we were married. It is an old Mexican land grant ranch that goes way back to the Elias family. It was abandoned two or three times during the times of the Apache raids. It wasn't until the Apache situation eased up that it became more of a stable operation. It is owned by the Brophy family of Phoenix now. It is still a big place—thirty-six thousand acres. It is unique because it is all patented. It doesn't have any state land or national forest land or BLM [Bureau of Land Management] land. It is also unique because Babocómari Creek runs almost the entire length of it, so water is available throughout the entire ranch. Obviously, that's why it was settled in the first place.

After we were married, I also worked construction for seven months. The money was great, but I had to travel throughout the state, so I elected to quit and stay with agriculture so that I could stay with the family. And I've never regretted that decision. I haven't made much money, but I've had a great life as far as security goes. We had the good fortune to meet the Mellor family, who gave me a job on the Canelo Hills Ranch, and that gave us the opportunity to raise our kids in the country. We have five children—Joe, Veronica, Amalia, Marcia, and Roxanna. When you live in the country, you have built-in control; you don't have your children roaming around in the streets. We were very progressive with our children as far as letting them be involved in school activities even though it meant we had to drive them into town often. I think that a lot of children who are raised in the cities don't have enough responsibilities, actual chores instead of just sports and school activities. We were also able to involve our children in 4-H. They learned animal husbandry and horsemanship. They raised lambs, pigs, calves, and horses and could sell some of their projects at fair time and make a little money. So they were learning while they were at home as well as at school! It also helped them later when they were applying for college scholarships.

As I said, I went to work for Mr. Brophy at the Babocómari right after we were married. I was there for a couple of years, and then I was fired! At the time I was working there, there happened to be about five or six cowboys from Sonora who were also working there. I wasn't a cowboy. I was tending to the agriculture, irrigating, doing hay work, and maintaining roads. For some reason or another when Mr. Brophy came down, he decided it was time to clean house, so he let the whole crew go, including myself and the foreman. However, a week later he found out that I was the one that was doing the farming, and he wanted me to come back. Apparently, I was the only one who was being productive! There was also a little bit of shenanigans as far as taking a beef here and there across the line! I had already gotten another job, but he made me a standing offer that if I ever needed a job, I was welcome to come back. I guess he realized he made a mistake when he let me go!

I started working road construction again. I worked for several contractors. I did earth moving; I was a grease monkey; I worked with concrete. I was literally working day and night, eight hours with the dirt contractor and eight hours with the concrete guy. I was meeting myself coming and going, so I quit again to spend more time with the family.

After that, I wrangled dudes for a year at the Circle Z, one of the oldest guest ranches in the area. When I was dude wrangling, there used to be an old Mexican cowboy who worked at the Oak Bar Ranch. He was a maestro. He'd be on his way to check the cattle where Patagonia Lake is now, and if I saw him, I would get on a colt and ride with him. That's how I learned to be a cowboy. It was learning it by doing it! I remember, also, another old cowboy I used to visit with. He was from Mexico, a *pueblito* called La Mesa, close to Imurís. He worked a lot of years here in the States and at a lot of big ranches around here. He was working at the former Miller Ranch. The old man lived by himself, and I used to go and visit him coming home from work. In the evening I'd go and have a cup of coffee with him; he really appreciated the visit. He was already eighty-five years old, and he'd be out there shoeing a horse! It was a difficult thing for him. The stories that I used to enjoy were the stories of the real cowboy experiences in Sonora. I wish that I had recorded those stories because now they have been lost.

In 1960 I had the opportunity to come and work for Mr. Clinton Mellor at the Canelo Hills Ranch, and I remained there for eighteen years. The Mellors were mainline people from Philadelphia. For the first five or six years there was a cattle operation, and then they sold their allotment, and we went strictly into the quarter horse business. I was showing horses quite a bit on the horse show circuit, and I was also taking a lot of outside horses to train. I was training horses for the San Rafael Valley Ranch. I also had a horse-shoeing business and had quite a few contracts. I also drove the school bus for sixteen years and tended bar at the Crossroads in Sonoita. It's been a life of work!

Speaking of the San Rafael Valley Ranch, it also has quite a history. It was an old Mexican land grant ranch also. Have you ever read the book by Diana Hadley

Joe Quiroga is a foreman and vaquero on the Diamond C Ranch in Elgin, Arizona. Photo by José Galvez (2002).

about the San Rafael Valley? A man named Colin Cameron came into the area in the late 1800s. He was tough on the homesteaders that he found there. He'd do almost anything to get the land. He didn't let anything stand in his way, and the judges were often on his side and gave him free rein for abuse. He ran off the people who were legitimately there.

While I was working for the Mellors at Canelo, they built a house on the ranch for us in 1961, and we've been living out in the country ever since. But I was over-extended as far as work is concerned. While I was working for Clinton Mellor, a man from Colorado bought part of the ranch where we are now, and I managed it for eight years. He was from Castle Rock and would come only once or twice a year, so I pretty much had to do everything. He wasn't a great believer in spending a lot of money on the place, so I had to use my own horse and cut my own posts when I was tending fences. I used a lot of creativity! I can be pretty resourceful; that's the way I grew up! I used to have to hustle! I've always worked for somebody, but I've always treated things as if they were my own.

As I said, I was overextended as far as work is concerned and was negotiating for another job with the Research Ranch so that I could eliminate some of the time going from one job to another. I was in the process of agreeing to go to work with the Research Ranch when Mr. Jelks came in and asked to talk to me for a moment. He asked if I would be interested in staying on and working for him on the ranch I had been running for Jim Lagae, which he had just purchased. I agreed to stay on and that was in 1975.

The ranch that Mr. Jelks purchased was a small place, about four sections. But a year later he purchased another six sections, all of what had been part of the original Houston ranch. At the time Mr. Jelks purchased the ranch, it was in a state of degradation, with a lot of bare ground and active erosion taking place. His first concern was to try to reverse what was happening. We used Lee Kuhn to do a lot of ripping on the mesa and eliminate some of the mesquite that had invaded a good portion of the ranch. Lee's work did not cause much improvement for the next two years as the drought continued for two or three more years.

I believe that it was in 1978 when we heard of Allan Savory and Holistic Range Management. Holistic Range Management [HRM] takes into consideration domestic animals, the wildlife, the riparian areas—the whole flora and fauna. At that point all of us—Mr. Jelks Jr., his family, and I—attended several school sessions on HRM that were being offered in Albuquerque, New Mexico, by Mr. Savory. Allan had developed the HRM concept as a game ranger and was a very observant fellow, and he began to notice that the vast herds of animals would absolutely trample the ground to a pulp. But they would remain in an area for only a very short time and then move on. They would basically disturb the first two millimeters of the soil, and though it looked severe, it was actually a tilling! With the proper rest, the soil would come out with much more energy because of the dunging, urination, and salivating. He didn't find the key to making it work well until he found the element of time control. The key was the short duration that the animals stayed in one place. By the time they made the rotation, the grass was refurbished.

The Holistic Range Management Center in New Mexico is the place where the material is coordinated and disseminated. It is practiced all over the world now. I went to school in New Mexico for several weeks to learn the method. I actually got to study with Allan Savory, the guru himself! If it's managed right, it can actually double your production. However, if you're careless with it, you can ruin the land in half the time. It takes a lot of biological planning and observations.

In the traditional type of ranching the same pastures will get two, three, four months of grazing in the same cycle. But with HRM on the unit, our grazing periods seldom exceeds two weeks for the year.

There was an analogy made at school of an old man at the top of a hill and a creek at the bottom of the hill. Every single day for thirty days the old man goes down the hill to the creek for a bucket of water and then goes up the trail. You can do that, or you can use 365 burros in one day to get the water you need for the year. You'll find that, in fact, although the impact of 365 burros in one day looks severe, it is not as severe as the erosion that takes place when you go back and forth every day for 365 days! The initial impact of the burros heals over more quickly!

The cattle under HRM have gotten more manageable. You can easily move seven hundred head of cattle with a whistle. You go to the gate and whistle, and they'll all come because they know that their reward is fresh pasture. You don't have to get on your horse and round up for hours at a time. You can see all your cattle every day in a matter of hours, compared to riding all day and seeing maybe 30 percent of them.

We have interchanged with some ranchers in Mexico who are involved with HRM. Once a year we try to meet with the Mexican ranchers who are participating and share ideas and techniques that are working the best for us. The Mexican ranchers are very creative, and the beauty of it is that everyone, the landowner as well as the peon, has a vested interest in the landscape goal.

I learned something very interesting when we were touring a ranch in Mexico. We came to this area that was totally denuded of any vegetation due to past management practices. The rancher had put some stock salt on the ground, and I suggested that if he put the salt in a feeder, it would be more economical. He told us that he had found out that if he left the salt directly on the ground, even long after the salt is gone, the cattle will come defecate in the area. Leaving the manure as organic matter and fertilizer will enhance the medium to establish new seedlings, which will reverse the degraded conditions.

We generally run five hundred head of cattle, but because of the drought and the fire we are down to two hundred head. It's amazing how the cattle-ranching business has changed. We still contract cattle, which are weighed and sold at auction and taken to the stockyards in Marana and Willcox. But you're talking the expenses of commuting, yardage, insurance. Nowadays a lot of cattle buying is done over video satellite that is seen all over the country on monitors! The cattle pass through and are bid on and identified by the local cattle mark.

This HRM method has opened up a lot of avenues for me. Right now the boss's son and another man are tending to the cattle. I help them when they're going to move the cattle from one ranch to another or when they have a sick animal, because I'm the cowboy. But now I spend most of my time doing watershed management. I've built literally thousands of rock structures up in the canyons and the hills.

The first structures that I built were in a steep canyon that was down to bedrock and looked like a rock slide! I built the rock structures in terraces, and in one year the silt had collected behind the structures, and grass was actually growing there! The terraces slow the water down and slow the movement of the soils and allow them to be revegetated.

I enjoy the hard physical work. I move rocks that weigh five, six hundred pounds by myself. People say they don't know how I do it! I feel that what I'm doing is important for the health of the land. The land has been damaged over the last century, and now it has a chance to heal. That's why I'm so enthusiastic about it. I feel that what I'm doing is important in the long term.

Over the years we have seen a lot of changes in the area. There's been a lot of development in Patagonia, Sonoita, and Elgin and a shift in the rural lifestyle. There aren't that many cattle here now; the horses that you see are mostly for recreational riding. Many folks are commuters or have weekend places. Land is now twice the price that it used to be, and there aren't that many people involved in agriculture. We used to know everyone, but now we don't. Not too long ago we went to a community play in Patagonia, and we hardly knew a soul!

We have a little house in Patagonia and a lot with a mobile home where our son lives with his family. But Noemi doesn't want to move back to the "big city"! We bought fifteen acres with our two daughters here on the border of the Diamond C Ranch as an investment. We also run a small herd on the Diamond C, and Noemi drives the school bus for fun.

I've been doing ranch work for over forty years, and I love my work. I don't ever intend to retire. I'm satisfied with my life and happy with my situation. I intend to work until the day I die. I love the animals, and I love being out. I never have been an indoor person, and I've always been a morning person. I'm gone by six thirty. I've never been a time waster. I try to get my hours in. I like to see my tracks; I want to know where I've been and what I've accomplished. Speaking of the work ethic, I've always set goals for myself, and I always exceed them, and that's been the story of my working life.

I'll stay here at the Diamond C as long as they allow me to. Noemi belongs to the Cowbelles, and I am a member of the Southern Arizona Cattleman's Association, both of which promote the cattle industry. We've made a lot of friends in the area. Our bosses, Keri and Rukin Jelks, have been extremely good to us, treating us as part of their family, and we hope to remain on the ranch as long as circumstances allow us to do so. Mr. Jelks is getting older and is having physical problems. He has a hard time getting around and doing the day-to-day things. I see myself looking after him and his wife in their old age. Even if I were totally disassociated with the cattle business, I wouldn't mind that. We're happy here in our little corner of the Diamond C Ranch.

Joe Quiroga herds cattle as part
of his job as a vaquero on the
Diamond C Ranch outside
Elgin, Arizona. Photo by José
Galvez (2002).

➡ One summer, while vacationing in the White Mountains in northern Arizona, I noticed a man sitting and reading on the front porch of a small log cabin. There were several family members around, including young adults and children. He greeted us, and because he seemed friendly, we stopped to chat. The book he was reading was *Land Use History of the San Rafael Valley* (1995), coauthored by Diana Hadley and Thomas E. Sheridan. I learned that Joe Quiroga and his wife, Noemi, have lived in the Patagonia-Elgin-Sonoita area of southern Arizona all of their lives and that Joe has spent most of his life working on ranches. My first interview with him took place in June 1997, and a second on November 22, 1997. My husband, Jim, and I have visited with Joe and Noemi a number of times, not only in Elgin, but also in the White Mountains. They have helped us to understand and appreciate their strong sense of family values as well as their passion for the land and the environment in which they live.

Agatha Cota Gastellum and
Luis Acuña Gastellum in their
eastside Tucson home. Agatha
holds a picture of herself and
her siblings when they lived
on the family ranch near
Tumacacori, Arizona. Photo
by José Galvez (1998).

Agatha Cota Gastellum

I was born in Tumacacori, Arizona, on August 22, 1914. My father's name was Francisco Cota, and my mother's name was Lucinda López. My paternal grandfather's name was Tomás Cota; he was from Baja California, Mexico. My paternal grandmother's name was Petra Grijalva; she was from Ures, Sonora, Mexico. My paternal grandfather homesteaded here in Tumacacori in the 1880s, and my father was born in the house his father built—the same house that I was born in! The main house in Tumacacori in which my father and all of us children were born in is still there, but it has changed. He would not recognize it! It has been plastered, so the adobe walls do not show up any more. Parts have been added and parts removed, and it has a different roof.

My mother, Lucinda López, was born in Greaterville, Arizona, a mining town in the Santa Rita Mountains. Her father, George López, was born in Los Angeles, California. My maternal grandmother's name was Zeferina. I don't know exactly when they settled in the area because there is no written history. My mother used to tell us the story of her grandfather's sister. She was hanging out her wash on the line to dry when they were attacked by a band of Apache warriors. She hid her baby under the tin wash tub, but the Apaches managed to grab her by the hair. They tore off all her hair with a yank, but the baby was saved!

My father was a farmer. He had a little orchard around the house and grew grapes, peaches, apricots, quince, pomegranates, and other kinds of fruit that he experimented with. On his 160 acres he planted corn, beans, potatoes, tomatoes, garbanzos, fava beans, teparies, chile peppers, and watermelons. He grew things that the people in the area did not ordinarily grow, like pumpkins and sweet potatoes. He also had beehives and sold the honey and the produce to the military camp in Nogales, Arizona, which was a camp of black soldiers. He planted for our family as well as to sell, and then he would put the excess by the side of the

Left to right: Consuelo, Hope, and Agatha Cota (Gastellum) at the Cota family homestead in Tumacacori, Arizona (1920).

road for anybody to take. He would give his shirt off of his back if you wanted it. He was very generous until the day he died.

My job when we were on the farm was to gather the eggs every afternoon. The chicken coop wasn't too far from the house, and one day I went in, and there was a snake eating the eggs! I am scared to death of snakes, and I said, "Mother, I'll do anything, but I will not go into the chicken coop to gather eggs!" And she didn't make me; she did it herself. She wasn't too much of a disciplinarian.

My brother Tomás and I were the oldest, and we would follow my father when he was plowing, and we would drop the bean and corn seeds. And when he plowed up potatoes for harvesting, we would go and gather them and put them in baskets. We didn't have to do it, but we liked doing it. My father was very easy-going with us. He was not a disciplinarian either. All he had to do was give us a look, and we knew he meant business!

When I was a child, it seemed to me that our house was very big. There was a long living room with a fireplace on the south side and a kitchen and two bedrooms in the back. There was a separate building that was called a *despensa*–a storeroom–where my father put up the corn and beans and everything that he grew for the winter. My mother wanted running water in the house, and so my father bridged water from the well with a gasoline pump. He pumped the water into a big storage tank, and then he piped it into the kitchen. So we had cold running water!

My mother had been a schoolteacher in Alto, which is near the mining town of Greaterville. She taught us English from the very beginning, and so we grew up speaking both English and Spanish. When they closed the school in Alto, they gave our mother the textbooks and also the blackboards. Father mounted the blackboards in the living room of our house, and we had our lessons there. My brother and I also started school in Tubac, but I went for only a short time because I was left-handed and the teacher tried to make me change. But I couldn't do it! My knuckles were always sore because she would hit them with a ruler. My mother belonged to the school board, and she said, "I am taking my child out of school. I will tutor her at home." And she did! When I was in the third grade, they opened a little school in Tumacacori, just south of the mission. The teacher,

Mrs. Macklehannon, never tried to change me. She said that I was born left-handed and that that is the way I was going to be! I went to school in Tumacacori until I was in the fourth grade. Then my parents sold their homestead, and we moved to Tucson.

My parents met in Alto. My father used to take his produce to Alto and the mining camps nearby to sell. My mother's father was a miner, but they also raised goats. My grandfather, George López, was part German descent on his mother's side. He was very fair and blue-eyed. Heinz Fifty-seven variety! When my father first met my mother, she was fifteen years old, and he was seventeen. My mother said that when she saw him, she told her mother, "That is the man I am going to marry." And her mother said, "You're too young to think of marriage." And my mother answered, "But I'll be older some day!" My father would leave my mother a note under a rock every time he went over there to Alto, and that is how they corresponded. Eventually my mother's family invited him to come and have a meal with them, and they fell in love. They married when she was eighteen years old and he was twenty. They were married in 1911 at St. Ann's Church in Tubac by a young priest from Nogales, Father Duval. And then they settled at the Cota family homestead in Tumacacori.

My father wrote a love song for my mother when they were courting. He played the song for her on his violin:

No sé porque, me dictó el corazón
El amarte a ti con ardiente pasión.
Tu me dirás si merezco ese don.
Ese don que me encanta. Ese don que me anuncia
Mi salvación.
No quieras nunca, no, a otro mas que a mí.
Mira que yo te dí, todo mi amor a ti.
Y siempre te he de amar con todo el alma a ti.
Y siempre te he de querer no más a ti.

I don't know why my heart commanded me
To love you with such ardent passion.

Tell me if I merit the gift of your love.
The gift that enchants me; the gift that announces
My salvation.
Don't ever love anyone else but me.
See how I gave all my love to you.
And I will always love you with all my soul.
And I will never love anyone but you.

My paternal grandmother, Petra, lived with us all of the time. My paternal grandfather, Tomás Cota, was a peddler, and he used to go all over the place to sell produce. He traveled to Globe and Miami and all the mining camps. While he was gone, my father would take over the homestead. Our grandmother Petra was very loving. She helped my mother a lot and cared after us children.

My parents had seven children—Tomás, myself, Frank, Benjamin, Consuelo, and Hope. Mother, being a farmer's wife, was always very busy. She was a very good seamstress and made all of our clothes. She crocheted a lot. My sisters and I always had crocheted lace on our clothes. I still have saved some crocheted edgings that she made for our little petticoats and collars.

Our mother was always busy in the kitchen, cooking or making bread or the big Sonoran tortillas. She had a wood-burning stove with a tank on one side, and it was always filled with hot water. We had a couple of milk cows, and she made cheese. She dried vegetables—string beans, squash, and tomatoes. She'd reconstitute them in boiling water. They always butchered in the fall and made beef jerky. The beef is cut into thin strips and seasoned with salt and dried. She had a screened cage for drying meat to keep the flies off. We always had a few hogs and made *carne adobada* in the water. It is made with pork strips marinated in a chile sauce and then dried. They made the thick sauce out of dried chile peppers and lots of garlic and vinegar. Mother would hang the marinated meat on a line and then put dish towels on it to keep off the flies. It is delicious.

I remember my mother baking a lot. She used to make *tostadas*—cinnamon crisps. They are made with raised yeast dough. After the dough rose, Mother would pat it flat and sprinkle it with cinnamon and sugar and then bake it before it rose again.

She made *coyotas* [a Mexican sweet bread] out of pumpkin, *piloncillo* [hard brown sugar], and raisins. She would chop the piloncillo and add raisins and a little flour and that would be the filling. Mother also made empanadas with dried and fresh fruit. She used to dry peaches, apples, and apricots and have them ready for pies as well as empanadas. I remember a pie that she made. There were no lemons available, but she used to make a vinegar pie. My father loved it! She would make *bizcochuelos* [anise cookies] and Mexican wedding cookies when we celebrated our saints' days. We celebrated our feast days as just a family thing.

My mother and grandmother used *hierbas* [herbs] such as *manzanilla* [chamomile], *hierbabuena* [mint], and *sauco,* the blossom of the elderberry tree. They would give us elderberry tea when we had a fever, cold, or sore throat. It was soothing! Hierbabuena and manzanilla were used for stomachaches. Mother always had a little garden patch where she grew her herbs. She also grew oregano. Elderberry trees were very abundant along the river, but they're mostly gone now. She also used to gather the fruit and make *atole,* which is a thick pudding that she made with the juice of the berries of the elderberry tree. It is thickened with cornstarch and sugar, and after it cools, it solidifies. My husband's brother, Jim Gastellum, has a lot of elderberry trees on his property. We used to gather the fruit there because they're clean. You don't want the fruit from along the highway because they spray them, and the berries collect fumes and dust. They're toxic!

I remember that the Santa Cruz River near our home always had water in it, and we used to go there and gather watercress. Now you wouldn't do it because it is so polluted, and now there's no water in the river where we used to live! When we were going to school in Tumacacori, the teacher and the students would go down to the river to eat lunch. We'd pick the watercress and wash it in the river and eat it! My mother also used watercress as a salad. She would sprinkle vinegar and sugar on it, and that's the way we would eat it. It was delicious!

We picked wild greens called *bledo* [amaranth] and *verdolagas* [purslane]. All the other wild greens we called *quelites.* Our children and grandchildren love verdolagas to this day! I sauté onions, peppers or green chile, tomatoes, and garlic in olive oil. Then I add washed and trimmed verdolagas to the sauté and let them steam. When they are done, I add a little milk and cheese. We actually cultivate verdolagas here in our garden in Tucson!

When I was a little girl, the nuns used to come from Nogales to Tumacacori Mission to give catechism classes; the classes were in Spanish. There used to be a convent at the mission, on the east side. It had a little building where we were taught our catechism. It is the part that is now melted away. We would practice in the mission. The priest from Nogales would come only once a month to say mass in Tubac, and that is where I made my First Communion.

My mother and grandmother taught me a lot of prayers and all about the Catholic faith and how we were to make our First Communion and Confirmation. They had a home altar; a painting of the Virgen de Guadalupe was prominent. Mother had different statues–Santa Teresita, the Sacred Heart, the Holy Family. She always had candles that she would light on the saints' feast days. We always prayed at night before going to bed. I remember the prayers in Spanish. Now when I go to confession and I'm supposed to pray, I don't say the prayers in English–just in Spanish!

The feast day of San Juan was on June 24. He was the patron saint of rain, and the rainy season was supposed to start on his feast day. There were celebrations– horse races and dances. I especially remember the feast day of San Isidro, the patron saint of farmers. We prayed for rain and for a good harvest. People would sing and carry a statue or a picture of San Isidro from farmhouse to farmhouse. There were a lot of different hymns that the women would sing. At every farmhouse we would stop for refreshments and then proceed to the next farmhouse. There were actually five farms: the Bejaranos', the Andrades', Cenovio Villa's, Don Pedro Galisto's, and ours. Don Pedro used to be the one who organized the Holy Week festivities at Tumacacori Mission. The Bejarano home, like ours, is also still standing there in Tumacacori.

For the fiesta of San Isidro the farmers and their wives would also make *teswín,* a fermented corn drink, and *bizcochitos.* We lived closer to the railroad, and when the train would stop in Tubac to de-ice, my father would go over there and get ice, and Mother would make ice cream in two big hand-cranked ice cream freezers! Everyone like to come to our house on the Feast of San Isidro because we had ice cream and cookies. It was a special treat!

My father, Francisco Cota, was a fiddler. He used to play the violin for all the dances around Tubac and Tumacacori. His sister Dolores played the guitar, and one of my father's nieces, Tula Alday, used to sing. There was a man with a peg leg named Mr. Burruel who played the bass. The dances were called *jamaicas,* and everyone in the community gathered for the food and dancing and singing. Although I was too little to dance, I used to love to go and watch everybody else dance. We had a little Ford, and Father would load us all up–three children and my mother and, of course, his violin, and we'd all go to the jamaica. Men used to pay for dancing. It was ten cents a dance or a dollar for the whole evening! The money was used to pay for the musicians. The people danced the *chotis* [schottische], the *varsoviana,* waltzes, and the two-step–all the old-fashioned dances. They used to wet down the dirt in the patios and smooth it down until it was just like concrete, and that's where they danced!

My father learned to play the violin in this way. My grandfather Tomás had a friend who was a professor in Mexico. One time he came to visit my grandfather at the homestead. He had his violin with him, and he taught my father how to play. My father did not read music; he played by ear. When the professor left, he left my father the violin. I still have it. It is over one hundred years old!

One of the reasons that my parents decided to sell the homestead was because the new highway had taken a lot of our land, and the road was very close to our home. Life had become hard for the farmers. Also, my mother wanted to leave Tumacacori because there wasn't proper schooling there. We moved to Tucson, and my father got a job with the City Parks. It was gardening, and so he fell right into it! All the trees you see now in the parks–Reid Park, Hi Corbett, and the old main library–were planted by my father. He had a crew, a chain gang made up of winos and loafers who were thrown into the jail overnight. These are the people that my father took to plant the parks and to take care of them and keep Tucson clean. When Joel Valdez was city manager of Tucson, I'd ask him, "Joel, why don't you send the chain gangs out like they used to when my father was working for the city?" And he'd answer, "Civil rights, ma'am!"

After we moved to Tucson, I went to Davis School for a while, and then I was sent to my grandmother's in Santa Barbara to go to school. I would visit Tucson in the summers. I was young when we left Tumacacori, so I didn't miss the farm very much.

My husband, Luis, and I knew each other as children because our families were friends. We met again at St. Ann's Church in Tubac. By that time, Luis was working in Casa Grande for the National Park Service, and he used to come and visit his folks once a month. My sister and I worked at the Mallory Ranch one season—no guests, just family. My sister did the cooking, and I waited on the tables and made sure Mrs. Mallory had her meals in bed.

Luis and I had a long-distance courtship. My parents were very strict. We were married at the Tumacacori Mission in 1939 in a simple Catholic wedding. The church was packed; everybody we knew came to the wedding, invited or not! The church had no seating, and everybody had to stand. The reception was attended by just the two families, which was big enough!

Luis Acuña Gastellum and Agatha Cota Gastellum at their wedding at Tumacacori Mission (1939).

Steve Gastellum helps his
mother, Agatha Gastellum, as
they visit the home where she
was born near Tubac, Arizona.
Photo by José Galvez (2002).

We needed permission from the government to be married at Tumacacori Mission because it was no longer an active church. We needed permission also from our pastor to be married outside of our parish. I wanted Monsignor Duval to marry us because he had married my parents and had baptized my brother and sister and me. By that time, he had retired, but he came and married us anyway. I wanted to get married in the mission because I had lived down there and because Luis was working for the National Park Service. We had to go through a lot of red tape, but we finally got permission! I thought it was a beautiful wedding. We celebrated our fiftieth wedding anniversary there.

Before I was married, I worked at the telephone company as an operator and then at Dave Bloom and Sons, a men's clothing store in Tucson, selling on commission. I also went to the Arizona College of Commerce. But I never worked a day out of the house after I got married. I worked plenty at home with seven children!

🎞 In June 1998 I went to the home of Luis Acuña Gastellum and Agatha Cota Gastellum with the intention of interviewing Mr. Gastellum. In the course of the initial conversation I became interested in Mrs. Gastellum's quiet remarks and decided to interview her also. Mr. Gastellum passed away on March 14, 2000. Mrs. Gastellum's devoted children–Marie, Gloria, Ed (Luis Eduardo), Francis, Steve, Ben, and Richard–spend as much time with her as possible, and she often travels to visit them if they live out of state. Since the initial interview, I have spoken to Mrs. Gastellum over the phone a number of times and have visited her several times to review family photos. My last visit was in the fall of 2002.

Luis Acuña Gastellum and
Agatha Cota Gastellum. Photo
by José Galvez (1998).

Luis Acuña Gastellum

I was born in Tubac, Arizona, in 1915. My father's name was Santiago Gastellum. He was born in Tubutama, Sonora, Mexico, in 1883. My paternal grandparents' names were Manuel Gastellum and Gregoria Morales Ochoa. My father's mother was one-fourth Opata Indian. The Gastellum family originally came from the Basque area of Spain to Alamos, Sonora, in the 1700s and had been involved in cattle ranching and agriculture in the Altar Valley of Sonora for several generations.

My father, Santiago, settled in the Santa Cruz Valley, in Arizona, in 1898. He had visited the valley when he was young because his family had been trading in the area for many years. When my father first settled in the valley, he worked as a farmhand and a cowboy for the man who would later become his father-in-law, Luis Acuña.

My maternal grandfather, Luis Acuña, was born in Ures, Sonora, Mexico, in 1849 and came to Arizona about 1870, when it was still a territory. He married my maternal grandmother, Josefa Féliz, who had come to the area about the same time. They had two daughters—Josefa, who was born in Tucson in 1880, and my mother, Santos, who was born at their homestead in Tubac in 1886.

In 1882 my grandfather Acuña learned of the opening of land for homesteading near Tubac, and on September 22, 1882, he filed a claim that measured 120 acres. It included the rich bottomland of the Santa Cruz River. He began immediately to improve his claim. He built a two-room adobe house, stables, corrals, a well, fencing, and a chicken house.

In 1903 my father, Santiago, became the foreman at my grandfather's ranch and farm and married my mother, Santos, that same year. He told me that instead of working for just a salary, he was paid half of his earnings in a share of the calf crop, so he could start to accumulate his own ranch stock. In 1907 Father

Y y

Brand of Santiago Gastellum (Father)

Luis Acuña Gastellum at the
Acuña family homestead in
Tubac, Arizona (ca. 1918).

registered his Yy brand. A year or two after my parents were married, my father
also began to working as foreman for the cattle operation of Sabino Otero. Otero
ran cattle in different locations–from Florence to the north, to the Santa Rita
Mountains to the east, and to the Baboquívaris on the west. My father told me
that they branded about fifteen hundred calves a year! He worked for the Oteros
for about twenty years.

My grandfather Acuña, died in 1911, and my grandmother Josefa died in 1915.
They are both buried in the Tubac cemetery. All of their holdings, including land,
cattle, horses, and farm equipment, were divided equally between my mother
and her sister, Josefa Salcido. They were their only heirs. My mother registered
her brand in 1915. All of the cattle and horses that she inherited were branded
with the numbers 915, 15 being the year of registration. My grandparents' brand
was AF, which stood for Acuña-Féliz. I remember that when I was young I rode
a number of horses with that brand!

I was born in my parents' home on the Luis Acuña Homestead with Rosa Lim, the grocer's wife, serving as midwife. I was the fifth of seven children. There were four boys and three girls: Jim, Manuel, Alfonso, Frances, myself, Gregoria, and Hortensia. Meanwhile, my parents also homesteaded south of Amado.

When I was four years old, U.S. Marshals evicted our family from my grandfather's homestead. The eviction occurred at a very difficult time for my mother as she had just given birth to my youngest brother, Manuel. She developed complications and had to have surgery, which confined her to bed for several weeks. My aunt, Juanita Sierras, cared for my infant brother in the meantime.

The eviction created great turmoil as all of the livestock—horses, milk cows, hogs, chickens, and goats—had to be relocated. My father had to arrange for temporary storage for the personal belongings of our family. Generous friends and relatives took us in until my father could fix up a cottage he owned on land north of Reventon, more than five miles from Tubac. The settlers were never reimbursed one penny for the improvements they had made to their land. Our family's experience was not unique. My mother had attended the territorial school of Tubac in the 1880s, and her teacher, Mrs. Black, described her own eviction in this way: "Yes, they took my land away. My land looked like an auction yard. They put everything out of doors. The furniture, the dishes, everything. It was the most brutal thing I ever saw."

Instead of a five-minute walk to school, my sisters and brothers now had to commute for three hours to school. When I was six years old, I began riding the school buggy. Our school day was very long, and I stayed with my godmother, Nina Luisa Rojes, who lived across from the school, until my older brothers and sister got out of class. Our cousins, Manuel and Josefa Salcido, also came to school in buggies from Amado. We left our horses in the stable of Raymundo Rojes. There were a lot of other Mexican families whose children went to school in Tubac—I remember the Gómezes, Aldays, Gortarezes, Olivases, Oteros, Sierras, Valdezes, Megarízes, Gutíerrezes, Madrils, and Castros.

My oldest brother, Jim, used to tell the story of how once, when the Santa Cruz river was running, he missed nine days of school in Tubac because his horse could

A-F

Brand of Luis Acuña and Josefa Féliz (Maternal Grandparents). (Later inherited by Luis Gastellum's mother, Santos Acuña)

not cross from our father's ranch on the east side of the river! The old school-house in Tubac is now part of the Tubac Presidio State Park.

I learned later that Congress had given five 100,000-acre land grants to the Baca family in exchange for their large claims in northern New Mexico. John Watts, who was the Baca attorney, helped them choose the tracts. Baca Float Number Three included Tubac, Tumacacori, and Calabazas. Watts later bought the shares of sixteen of the seventeen heirs for sixty-eight hundred dollars!

As early as 1886, when my grandfather Acuña's application was first accepted, the U.S. Land Office had declared these lands open for homesteading. On July 9, 1896, President Grover Cleveland signed the Luis Acuña Homestead Certificate Number 751. I have in my possession certified copies of the original documents. Before my grandfather passed away in 1911, the possibility of eviction had already surfaced, but he felt that the government would not force out people who had patented claims. Up until his death my grandfather maintained faith that the government would in the end recognize all of the sacrifices he had made to settle the land legally. None of his heirs had agreed to any deal.

In 1988 the Bureau of Land Management told me that the Luis Acuña Homestead was never canceled or invalidated. The government should have informed my grandfather of the Supreme Court's decision and given him or his heirs the opportunity to file a protest prior to the eviction. If he did not file within five years, he then lost his right to redress. But the government never informed him of this.

After our eviction my father continued ranching and farming on our homestead north of Tubac, and I have a lot of fond memories from that time.

We boys had a lot of chores on the ranch and farm. We were responsible for helping our father with the cattle raising, and that included the jobs of branding and neutering calves and monitoring them for screwworms and infections. Our father was very skilled at neutering animals—everything from calves to hogs to colts. The neighboring ranchers would bring in their colts, and he would stable them for a few days to ensure that no infection would set in. As we grew up, he taught us with great patience other ranching skills such as repairing fences and looking for cattle lost on the range that had not come in for water.

Woodcutting and gathering were other important jobs that we had. We picked up dry mesquite branches and heavy stumps in the sandy washes that had been exposed by summer floods. We would bring it to the central woodpile and then separate it for the fireplace and the cooking stove. In the winter we hauled firewood and started the evening fires to heat the house.

We participated in the annual roundups. Our relatives and godparents sometimes joined in for as long as four days over an area covering twenty to thirty square miles. There was open range from the base of the Santa Ritas to the Salero Mountains and across the valley to the Tumacacori Mountains. That is when we learned about ranching—about branding, castrating, and culling out the best cows for butchering. At the end of the roundup we separated the six- to ten-month-old calves and some cows from the rest of the herd and drove them to the Amado train-loading facility, where buyers would look them over and offer a price. We would then drive the rest back to home pastures, a difficult chore since the cows kept mooing and wanting to return to look for their calves! By this time the cows were already pregnant with the following year's crop.

My father organized trading trips to Nogales and Tucson. My older brother Jim usually went with him, but when I was about ten years old, I went along to Tucson, a three-day trip! I helped load the wagon with sacks of corn and beans, chile *ristras* [strung chile], pumpkins, and bundles of corn husks for tamales. We began our trip early in the morning. We were heavily loaded. We traveled more than halfway the first day and camped near Continental, where dad found a nice grove of trees and running water. We harnessed the horses, fed them, and tied them up for the night. Early the next morning Dad made a campfire, brewed coffee, and made our breakfast. While he was doing this, I fed and watered the horses and brushed the dried sweat off of their backs. Then we harnessed the horses for the rest of the trip.

I remember the trip so well, especially the beauty of the valley, with its beautiful sunsets and morning skies. The Santa Cruz River was flowing with clear water for practically the whole trip.

When I was eleven years old, my father gave me a beautiful gray filly named Mora. When the filly was eighteen months old, my father told me it was time to break her in. We saddled her and led her into a sandy wash. There my dad let me mount her while he held the rope around her neck. She was nervous. I took the reins, but my dad used the rope to guide the filly and me at a trot and then a gallop. After we had trotted over the sand for a while, Dad removed the rope and told me to follow him, keeping the reins tight. We practiced turning from right to left. My filly and I rode together with my dad for a couple of miles before returning to the home barn.

My father was always very particular about his horses, and he taught us to be sure that our own mounts were always well fed and cared for. He constantly reminded us to brush and clean their backs because sweat and dirt would cake under the saddle. He was patient in training us, but severe with us if he noticed that we were not taking good care of our horses!

In 1926 our family bought a Model T Ford. Our life changed almost immediately! We went to Tucson more often, and we saw our first silent movies! We boys helped my dad brush the wagon trail, remove the rock from the roadway, and smooth out the Santa Cruz River crossing. The river kept changing course, and so new roadbeds had to be built!

Over the years my father, Santiago, became associated with various buyers of Mexican cattle. He would go down to Tubutama-Caborca-Pitiquito country, which he knew so well, and buy up large herds and drive them up to Arizona through the Altar Valley. In addition, at one point he worked as deputy sheriff for about six or seven years under Jay Lowe, who was a famous Santa Cruz County sheriff.

My father was known for his roping ability and for training horses for cattle work and for breaking horses. He competed in rodeos. At the 1926 Fiesta de los Vaqueros in Tucson he and his partners, Jim Kane and Jesús Ahumada, won prizes in team roping. One of his prizes was a Visalia silver-trimmed leather saddle that I rode on when I was a boy. Father competed professionally for fifty years and was noted for his heeling ability in team roping events. He often teamed with my brothers Al and Jim. He was eventually inducted into the Santa Cruz Cowboy Hall of Fame.

When he was eighty years old, my father gave a roping exhibition at a ranch just east of Nogales on the Patagonia Road. It is said that his ease and grace on a horse, even at that advanced age, were something to see! Two years later, on a Sunday morning, my brother Al came to his place to go to another rodeo. My father, however, died in his sleep about an hour before my brother's arrival, on January 6, 1965. He was to heel for Al that day. He literally died with his boots on! He was buried in the Tubac cemetery alongside our mother, who had died in 1962. When Mother died, he built a beautiful white chapel over her grave.

Our mother, Santos, was a very honorable and compassionate person. She had a very gentle character. Anything that hurt someone would make her cry! She kept the family united. She taught us our catechism, sewed our clothes, and healed us with her home remedies. The first time I was treated by a doctor was after we bought our first car in 1926! Mother was very industrious and a good homemaker. She dried and canned fruits and vegetables and made cheese and butter. My three older sisters were responsible for cooking and household chores and for milking the cows. They fed the chickens and pigs, gathered eggs, and hauled water from the well.

When I was about eleven years old, I would go to Tubac and Tumacacori on my gray filly to peddle cheese. Mother allowed us to exchange quesadillas for fresh vegetables from Manuel Guidacan, who owned two or three acres east of upper Tubac. He was the area's intensive truck garden farmer and raised crops during the four seasons of the year! Isidro and Sofía Otero also had a small orchard. They planted a row of beautiful quince trees along the frontage road to their house. In the fall, when the fruit would ripen, I would exchange quesadillas and white cheese for the fruit. Mother would always make quince jam. The Oteros had the best quince in the valley!

Saints' days were important celebrations. On San Juan's Day, the twenty-fourth of June, our *tía* Juanita hosted family reunions and served *teswín* [a fermented corn drink] and *barbacoa* [barbequed meat]. Santa Ana was the patron saint of our village church in Tubac, and there was always a special mass that day. El Día de Santiago on July 25 was the saint's day we celebrated most in our home because it our father's saint's day. Friends and relatives came to visit. This was the favorite day for horse racing, and we used the word *Santiago* to start the races. The Spaniards had used that word as their war whoop while engaging the Moors in battle, so it was a very old tradition!

There were also large get-togethers for wakes. Embalming was unheard of because of the isolation of the area, and so the minute a person died, messengers on horseback would spread the word that a wake would be held that very night. Family and friends made food and came to the nightlong vigil. A ring of coals would be made in the open patios to keep the food warm until the midnight supper. The men would sit around the fire, and the women would pray over the deceased inside the house. If the priest could not come to say mass, the women would lead the funeral prayer before the burial.

During Holy Week before Easter an Opata or Yaqui Indian and the Catholic ladies from the Tumacacori area led a special passion program at Tumacacori Mission. The celebration began on Holy Thursday, when the adult men, dressed as the Pharisees, visited homes throughout the valley begging for food. In the evening everyone would gather for prayers and plays about the events of Holy Week. On Holy Saturday we celebrated the resurrection and punished the *fariseos* by whipping them with willow wands while they marched into the mission asking for forgiveness. When I was between eight and twelve years old, I participated as a whipping member of the youth brigade.

Horse racing was very popular. At least twice a year the best horses in the valley would be matched against their equals. When I was about ten years old, my brother Jim and I went with our father when he took three horses from the Tumacacori Mountains to a race in Arivaca. There were picnics, dancing, football games, and a mass at the chapel. One famous horse race took place in Tubac. It matched El Alazán, owned by Santiago Lowe, to El Rayado, owned by Rosario Valenzuela. People in the Santa Cruz Valley who owned good race horses included the Megaríz family, Santiago Lowe, Tirso Trujillo, and Evaristo Gómez.

One of the most pleasant things I remember about my youth were the good schools in Tubac. I especially remember my teacher, Miss Josephine Cotter, who taught me in the second and third grade. She taught religion classes after school and was a pianist and had us participate in schools and songfests. I remember also Mr. Williams, the teacher and principal of the upper grades. He conducted spelling bees and math contests.

In 1929 my cousin, Mary Stella Rosenberg, and I enrolled in high school in Nogales and finished in three and one-half years! In 1935, two days after my graduation from the Arizona College of Commerce, I went to work for the National Park Service, from which I retired in 1973 from a high executive position. In 1939 I married Agatha Cota, whose parents and grandparents were also homesteaders in the Tumacacori area at the turn of the century. They also lost one of their patented homesteads to the Baca Float interests.

By 1925 most of the evicted homesteaders had settled elsewhere. Many of them left the Santa Cruz River Valley for cities or became migrant workers who followed the harvests. After World War II many of the Mexican American families with small plots of land were bought out, and the small farms all but disappeared.

Luis Acuña Gastellum with his "courting car" in Tubac, Arizona (ca. 1935).

Only two members of our family, my brother Jim and a grandchild raised by my parents, Yolanda Aros, have retained an interest in ranch life.

My brother Jim still lives in Tumacacori and follows in my father's footsteps. His life has been mostly ranching, farming, and team roping. And his children, grandchildren, and great-grandchildren carry on as horseback riders and team ropers. When he was already up in age, he won a team roping contest with his grandson Tony. He worked at many of the ranches in the area when he was young, including Rancho Canto, which belonged to Teófilo Otero. At one time he also worked for the Baca Float Ranch before it became the Río Rico development, and he was the manager of the El Canto Ranch at the Santa Gertrudis Crossing, which was owned by the president of Eastman-Kodak. His wages were a house, utilities, and 250 pounds of beef cut and wrapped every three months, plus 10 percent of the gross sales! Although he also worked for the Arizona Department of Transportation for more than twenty-five years, he still ran his own cattle, which he kept at the PM Ranch in Tubac until 1992. Since his retirement he keeps busy with his hobbies, making bits and bridles for horses, roping dummies, and inventing different kinds of tack!

I cannot help but feel nostalgic for the beauty and the spirit that prevailed in the valley when I was young. The giant cottonwood trees and thick willow groves have disappeared from the Santa Cruz Valley because of the water being pumped by the mines, and the big cash crop farms have replaced the truck gardens of the original settlers. It was a time when one could freely travel the horse-and-wagon trails that linked the valley. Few fences blocked the way, and gates could be easily opened and closed. The sense of community is completely gone now. I don't think that there is enough mingling of the old natives with the new people coming in. The old families are completely out of the picture.

Development continues to take place on the land that was stolen from the homesteaders and that continues to attract Anglo retirees. One of the subdivisions south of Tubac is mostly within the homestead once owned by my grandfather, Luis Acuña. Unfortunately, the State Park Boundaries failed to preserve and protect the four-room Acuña house. The abandoned building remained intact until recently, when the owners allowed the Tubac Fire Brigade to destroy it in a practice drill.

➤ In the fall of 1997 I attempted to interview Mr. Santiago (Jim) Gastellum, who was a cowboy and rancher of some fame in the Tumacacori area. He was in a great deal of discomfort at the time owing to arthritis, so he referred me to his brother Luis, who had written an article about the Gastellum family history that had appeared in the *Arizona Journal of History* (July 1995, pp. 1–31). I visited Luis Gastellum and his wife, Agatha, in their home in Tucson in June 1998. Luis also was ill at the time, and speaking at any length caused him to have coughing spells. I was able, however, to record a partial interview on which a small part of this chapter is based. This chapter is adapted in large part from the article that Mr. Gastellum wrote for the *Arizona Journal of History*. It is reprinted here with permission of the Arizona Historical Society and Luis Acuña Gastellum. Mr. Gastellum passed away on March 14, 2000. His brother, Santiago, passed away in 2002.

Ramón de la Ossa's hands.
Photo by José Galvez (2002).

Ramón de la Ossa

I was born in Nogales, Arizona, on August 27, 1946, the youngest of twelve children. My brother Eduardo and I were the only ones of my parents' children that were born in a hospital. All of my other brothers and sisters were delivered in Lochiel, Arizona, by a midwife. My father, Rosamel de la Ossa, was born in Lochiel, Arizona, on March 22, 1896, and died at the age of ninety-three on May 18, 1989. My mother, Mercedes Ramírez, was born on September 24, 1904, in Hermosillo, Sonora, Mexico, and died at the age of sixty-seven on November 15, 1971.

My paternal grandfather, Antonio de la Ossa, was the first de la Ossa to settle in Lochiel here in the San Rafael Valley. He was born in El Encino, California, in the San Fernando Valley in 1838 and died on my dad's birthday in 1902.

My great-grandfather's name was Vicente de la Osa. The spelling of the family name was changed from one *s* to two, but we're not sure why. Don Vicente came from the Basque area of Spain and settled in California before it became part of the United States. He was married to Rita Pérez de Guillén. In 1842 and 1843 he acquired a land grant for a ranch called La Providencia, which is now where Burbank and Forest Lawn are. Then he acquired another grant for Los Encinos. The title was approved in 1851. He raised cattle and sheep there and built a large home of eleven rooms with thick adobe walls. He and my great grandmother raised fifteen children there. The ranch was very large—about five thousand acres. For some reason or another he came on hard times and sold part of his holdings, and their children began moving out to different places. Part of my great-grandfather's holdings became state land, and now the old de la Osa ranch house at Los Encinos is a museum in a California State Park. It is located just outside of Los Angeles in Encino, California, on Balboa and Ventura Avenues and is open to the public to tour. It has the history of my family.

During one of the recent California earthquakes—I think it was in 1986—some of the walls of the buildings at the ranch house museum were cracked and damaged. While it was being restored, the groundskeeper stole out of the old house most of the original antique furniture that had belonged to my great-grandparents.

I was real impressed when I visited there. Sometimes I think back—I wonder how it would have affected me if I had lived in those days. I try to imagine how they lived and what they went through. It must have been really something to be a cowboy or rancher during the time of the Californios. I know that my dad visited the family home at Los Encinos at one time. And our house in Lochiel—the one my dad built—is identical to the house in California. You look at our house, and you see the same house, except our house is much smaller!

When Don Vicente came on hard times, my grandfather, Antonio de la Ossa, and one of his brothers, Abel, went into the freight business. In 1880 they came into this area of southern Arizona and hauled freight for the mines and the railroad. They were headed to Guaymas, Mexico, but the story is that my grandmother, whose name was Carolina Yanos, got tired of traveling. They already had three children, who had been born in California, and traveling was a hardship. So she insisted they stop here. At that time, Lochiel was known as La Noria, which means "waterwheel." Another family story is that they thought they were already in Mexico when they settled here and didn't find out that they were in the United States until the border was surveyed a few years later! My grandparents eventually had thirteen children. My father, Rosamel, was the second to the youngest.

There had been a homestead act in 1864, and my grandfather Antonio applied for a homestead. He started his cattle business with thirty heifers he bought in Mexico. The de la Ossa brand was OSA with an open A. He was cattle ranching in this area before Arizona became a state. It was all open range in those days, and he grazed his cattle on both sides of the border. He made a very good living selling beef to all the mines in the Patagonia Mountains. He also drove his cattle to Tombstone and Nogales after the towns were founded. Sometimes they would even drive a team of horses to Tucson to buy supplies. It took one day to get there, but three to get back because of the load they carried!

O S Λ

Brand of Antonio de la Ossa
(Grandfather)

My grandfather Antonio also farmed and sold the produce that they grew to the storekeeper in Washington Camp. There was a large area by my grandfather's house where they had an orchard, and farther out there were fields where they grew their produce. They hired field hands to help them with the harvest and practiced dry farming, which depends on rain for irrigation. They also raised other animals like hogs, sheep, and chickens. My dad said that they hardly ever had to buy anything because they also grew their vegetables, like potatoes, carrots, lettuce, beans, tomatoes, and chile for the family's use.

I recall my dad telling me that his father used to have to fight off the Apache Indians and outlaws. There are some big old cottonwood trees that are still alive by our house in Lochiel. My dad used to tell me that when he was about four years old, he remembers his dad would camp under those cottonwoods and sleep in a buckboard looking after his cattle with a rifle so that the rustlers wouldn't come and steal them! Sometimes the outlaws would come by the headquarters and demand to be fed and housed until they were rested up!

They struggled to keep their land. At one time there was a man in the valley called Colin Cameron who owned the San Rafael Valley Ranch. He was from the East. He was hard to deal with, and he pushed all the little guys out of the valley so that he could possess their land. He ousted and drove out all the small operators, but he couldn't budge my grandfather, Antonio de la Ossa! At one time in the late 1800s there was also a bad drought. All of my grandfather's cattle died except one head, and he had to start all over!

As I mentioned, when my grandparents came to Arizona from California, they already had three children—Clotilde, Alberto, and Abel. Abel was the father of my oldest cousin, Abel Jr., who just died a few months ago at the age of eighty-six. My grandparents at first lived in a house that was already here when they arrived, and later on my grandfather built a large house for his family at the turn of the century. It is the original de la Ossa ranch house, and it is still standing. It was restored by my father's sister, my aunt Marie, and now it belongs to my cousins Ed Roberts and Rosemary Miller. My father was probably born in that house.

My grandfather, Antonio de la Ossa, died in 1902, when he was chasing a steer and his horse stepped into a gopher hole and threw him. He got back on his horse and made it back to the house, where he died a short time later. My grandmother Carolina never married again. In those days women always wore black after they were widowed. They were *de luto,* in mourning. And from what I understand, the pigmentation and texture of her skin was affected from wearing black for so many years!

After my grandmother Carolina was widowed, she continued ranching, and she filed for her own homesteads. She eventually owned three. Some of the other children—Clotilde and Abel, Ernesto and Osvaldo—also homesteaded at the same time that my grandmother did, so there was a lot of de la Ossa land here at one time. I recall my father telling me that when the government passed the Homestead Act, they all piled into a buckboard and rushed to Nogales to file their homestead papers! My father didn't file for his homestead, but he inherited some deeded land and lease land from his mother, Carolina, when she died. The families were large, and some of the land has been divided into smaller parcels, but it's still mostly in the family. My cousin Abel was the only one who sold.

My grandmother Carolina filed for her homesteads and was managing the ranch with the help of some of the older children. At one time, I am told, she had a remuda of more than one hundred head of horses, so you can imagine the number of cattle she must have had! Probably four or five hundred head. She was pretty prosperous at one time as she continued in my grandfather's footsteps and continued selling the beef from her cattle to the mines in the Patagonia Mountains—Harshaw, Duquesne, Washington Camp, the Trench Mine, which was called "El Tranchee" by the Spanish speaking people. There were people galore in this area when the mines were active, so she had a lot of business.

My father used to tell me about those days. He said they would put the meat in a buckboard and go to the mining towns to deliver it and come back in the middle of the night. His mother would wear a hat and light up a cigarette so that the outlaws would think she was a man!

My father used to tell me that his mother was a go-getter. She was in business to stay in business. Before my grandfather Antonio died, they were pretty prosperous, and they began sending their sons to St. Michael's College in Santa Fe, New Mexico. After my grandmother became a widow, she continued sending them to college through her hard work. As a matter of fact, I have a certificate of excellence for English that was awarded to my father from St. Michael's College that is dated 1915!

My father worked as a ranch hand for his mother until he got sent off to college in Santa Fe. In his second or third year she called him back to the ranch to help her because she was having problems and was losing the ranch. She lost one of her leases in the Duquesne to the Hathaway and Steen families and had had a large herd of cattle stolen by rustlers. So my father returned to help his mother, and he set the pace for her and got her out of debt. It was difficult to run a ranch in those days, let alone for a woman! It was so isolated. But my grandmother Carolina was a survivor, and she pulled through. My father used to tell me that his mother was a very hard woman, not only with discipline, but also as a businesswoman. When he left school to help her, she didn't pay him what she should have. But he stuck with her until she passed away.

My aunt Marie was the youngest daughter, and she didn't marry until after my grandmother died so that she could take care of her. When Carolina died in 1938 at the age of eighty-two, my father and my aunt Marie inherited the three homesteads almost equally. Besides the private land, my dad inherited a permit for seventy head of cattle, and my aunt inherited a permit for sixty-two head. Right now I have 2,340 acres of forest lease. My grandmother had almost double that!

My mother, Mercedes, and my father, Rosamel, met through one of his older brothers, Osvaldo. Osvaldo was married to Teresa Cervantes, who was my mother's aunt. When my mother was fourteen years old, she came to visit Lochiel with some of her aunts, and that's when she met my father for the first time. They didn't get married until nine years later, after he returned from St. Michael's College in New Mexico.

When my mother and father were first married, they lived in a little house that was on my aunt Clotilde's homestead. My father saved his money, and he built our house in 1940. He built our house on my aunt's homestead because he liked the view from the hill. So now the house belongs to me, but the property doesn't.

As you can imagine, it was really hard to raise twelve kids. My mother was always busy with household chores–cleaning, washing, and cooking. There was

Rosamel and Mercedes de la
Ossa *(center)* at their wedding
in Hermosillo, Sonora, Mexico
(January 15, 1928).

Rosamel and Mercedes de la Ossa *(center)* with family and friends at the de la Ossa homestead in Lochiel, Arizona, in the San Rafael Valley (ca. 1950).

no electricity or gas, and she cooked all of our meals on a wood-burning stove. They didn't get electricity until 1967! She had to heat the water on the stove to do her wash, and she used one of those irons that is heated on the stove as well. It would take a whole day to get to Nogales in a buckboard to buy staples, although later on my father did buy a truck. When we'd get sick, she'd nurse us back to health with one of her home remedies. If we got gravely ill, she would take us to see Dr. Rosete in Santa Cruz, Sonora, just across the border. They raised a lot of their own vegetables in a field that is just below the house. In fact, Dad told me that during the depression, which was before I was born, they never went without food because they raised everything themselves! Mother canned meat and vegetables and fruit; they had a *subterráneo* [cellar] where they used to keep the food they preserved. She also raised chickens, turkeys, guinea fowl, and ducks. We didn't have a chicken coop. The hens laid their eggs in the tall grasses and in the woodpiles, and Mother trained them to roost in trees so that the coyotes and bobcats couldn't get them!

   In spite of all the hard work my mother had raising twelve children, she did have a beautiful garden until the day she died. She had all kinds of flowers. You name it, she had it—roses, gladiolas, mums! She even won prizes for her roses at the Santa Cruz County Fair! I don't know how she made time for gardening with all us children to raise. My father was a rancher and cowboy and wasn't around a lot of the time. But she made time. I guess it was a kind of therapy for her.

The women in the family were very religious. One of our cousins, Felicitas, who was married to one of our older cousins, Alberto, taught all of us children our prayers and catechism. When the priest would come, he would say mass in the home of my aunt Teresa, Uncle Osvaldo's wife. In 1958 our family built the chapel here in Lochiel. They contributed money as well as their labor. They did the actual construction and also bought all the saints for the chapel. The original name of the chapel is the San Antonio, but everyone calls it the de la Ossa chapel. The priest from Patagonia used to come and say mass here, but now the diocese of Tucson has given it back to the family. It is not recognized as a consecrated church in the diocese anymore. Now it's mostly used for family funerals.

There was a schoolhouse in Lochiel when I was growing up. The school building as well as the house that the teacher used to live in are still standing. There were a lot of families in the area because of the mines. In fact, there used to be a dance every Saturday night in Harshaw. All the cowboys and miners would go! Although our father spoke English well, our mother didn't, so we didn't know English when we went to school. The teacher was Anglo and didn't speak Spanish, and it was a hardship, but we got along.

All of us kids helped out at the ranch with the chores and the branding and the roundup. A lot of us had summer jobs at some of the neighboring ranches in the area. There was the Heady Ashburn Ranch and the Mowry Ranch and then us—right next to the border. We were the only Mexican family here in the early days and are the only Mexican family that is still ranching. But we didn't experience any prejudice that we can recall. You see, they depended on us for their labor.

One of the biggest ranches in the area—it is all private land—is the San Rafael Valley Ranch. It was a Mexican land grant at one time, and then it became the property of Colin Cameron, whom I spoke about earlier. Colonel Greene, who had the mines and ranches in Cananea, Mexico, bought it from Cameron. His grandson, Bob Sharp, just sold it to the Nature Conservancy, who in turn sold

Ramón de la Ossa sits in the chapel built by the de la Ossa family in Lochiel, Arizona, on the U.S.– Mexico border. Photo by José Galvez (2002).

most of it to a private individual. Part of the San Rafael Valley Ranch–the old ranch house built by Cameron and 3,500 acres–is now a state park.

My dad used to have supplemental jobs as much as he could in addition to ranching. He worked for the county on the roads, and he helped with roundups at the neighboring ranches. I think he could have managed without working on the side, but he did it to keep himself more occupied. Earlier on he used to sell his cattle commercially to cattle buyers who'd come out to the ranch with a semi

R̄
9

*Brand of Rosamel de la Ossa
(Father) and Ramón de la Ossa*

and haul the cattle out. Later on he started taking them in to the livestock auction in Tucson. He'd hire a truck to take the cattle in to the sale, like I do now. His brand was R Bar 9 (open 9), which I have now.

As the years went by, all of us kids started growing up and leaving the valley. I joined the navy and served in Vietnam on a minesweeper, the *U.S.S. Lucid,* which was part of the Seventh Fleet. I came back to Tucson and married my wife, Amy Dueñas, who is from Morenci. We have three children, Ramón Jr., Josh, and a daughter, Tina. I worked at the Cypress Pima open-pit mine for many years, and on my days off I would go back to the ranch in Lochiel and help my dad.

I moved back to Lochiel full-time in 1983 because my dad was getting up in age, and he needed someone to take care of him and take over the ranch. My wife, Amy, learned to love it out there!

My dad grew up without a father. He had to learn things on his own, and so he thought, "My kids are going to learn things the hard way like I had to." He was a self-made man, and he expected his kids to be the same way. He wouldn't instruct us. For example, take shoeing a horse. He'd say, "There's the horse. Do it!" That's the type of man he was. But as he got older, he changed. After we moved back to the ranch full-time, I'd go in, and I'd ask him, "Dad, how do you do this? How do you do that?" And then he'd teach me. So that's when I did most of my learning–as an adult!

When we went back to the ranch to live full-time, we had to subsidize our income. I got a job as a ranch hand and foreman at the Santo Niño Ranch two years after I went back. I worked there for fifteen years–ten years with one boss and five years with another. Earl Hardy was the owner of the Santo Niño Ranch. He's a CPA from Cave Creek, Arizona. He's originally from Minnesota, and he had always dreamed of having a ranch, so he bought the Santo Niño and built a home there.

Amy is a stay-at-home mom and decided to get her license for foster care. She's been doing that for eighteen years. We've had dozens of kids. They'd send them from Nogales. I guess they thought that ranch life with the fresh air and countryside would be good for them! Some of those kids still come out to the ranch and visit us!

Amy de la Ossa prepares a
caldo (soup) for her husband,
Ramón, and their daughter,
Tina, in the kitchen of their
ranch in Lochiel, Arizona.
Photo by José Galvez (2002).

Rosamel de la Ossa *(left)* and Ramón de la Ossa at the de la Ossa ranch in Lochiel, Arizona, in the San Rafael Valley. Photo by Jay Dusard, used by permission (1985).

When my father died, his homestead was split among our family. He had one and a half homesteads—about 240 acres. I inherited 160 acres, and all my brothers and sisters also inherited property. My brother Ed is an engineer and worked for oil refineries in California. When he retired, he built a home out here and has been living here full-time since last March. So the family is starting to come back to the valley now!

I was laid off from my foreman job at the Santo Niño Ranch. We've had a ten-year drought, and times are tough. That's the reality of ranching now. Our forest lease had allowed us to run seventy-nine head of cattle, but they've cut us back to fifty head. The government has a program called the Growing Smarter Program, where they subsidize you for the all the cattle that you've been cut back. Those twenty-nine cattle or so made a big difference in our income, so I've had to move back to Tucson to find a job. We have a house here that my dad bought for us years ago, and when we moved out to be with him on the ranch, we rented it out.

You asked about change. I'd say that the biggest change in Lochiel are the drug smugglers. We have problems with fences; we have problems with debris. They camp and leave a big old mess. They trash everything; they don't respect anything. I don't ever feel like I'm in danger, though. I've been riding the range and run across them with their big old backpacks. I go around them when I see them, and they don't bother me. . . . One time my brother and I ran across a transaction, and one of the kids ran toward us. He said, *"Hey, amigos. No más ando trabajando. Haciendo la vida"* [Hey, friends. I'm just working. Trying to make a living"]. And I said to myself, "I'm getting out of here!" And I rode on and never looked back!

Now that I'm back in Tucson, I go out to the ranch as often as I can. As soon as I retire, I'm going to go back there and live full-time. Before I moved back full-time to help my dad, ranching started getting in my blood. I started feeling that way shortly after my mother passed away. I would visit my dad, and even though he was getting older—he was seventy-six years old when Mother passed away—he was still pretty strong. He still rode horseback; he still roped and did all the ranch chores.

Anyway, it got in my blood, and I couldn't get rid of it. I got the feeling, "I want to do this!" It got so deep in my veins that I can almost taste it. I'll be on a horse riding the range, riding the fence line—all the duties of a rancher out in the open. It's an overwhelming feeling that I get in my mind and body. There's no turning back. Our oldest son, Ramón Jr., loves it out here, too. He wants to continue the ranching tradition of the de la Ossas.

I'm looking forward to retirement so that I can go back home to Lochiel permanently and stay there until I die. We have a family cemetery there above the chapel on the top of the hill. It overlooks the valley. I want to be buried in the family cemetery in Lochiel right beside my parents.

🐾 When I returned to my native state of Arizona in 1969, I visited the San Rafael Valley a number of times. I was entranced by its incredible beauty—the space of the land and the sky—and its history. I remember passing more than once the cluster of adobe houses in Lochiel and wondering who might have settled there. A few years ago I read *Land Use History of the San Rafael Valley* (1995), written by

Ramón de la Ossa locks up the family cemetery, which overlooks the San Rafael Valley. Several generations of de la Ossas are buried there. Photo by José Galvez (2002).

A scenic view of the San Rafael Valley, which looks out on the United States to the left and Mexico to the right. Photo by José Galvez (2002).

Diana Hadley and Thomas E. Sheridan, and I became intrigued with the de la Ossa historical importance in the San Rafael Valley. Diana Hadley helped me to locate Ramón de la Ossa after several failed attempts. He is living at the moment in Tucson, and I interviewed him in his home on October 30, 2002. I have also visited with him and his wife, Amy, on subsequent occasions, going over family photographs and history. I traveled with José Galvez to Lochiel and the San Rafael Valley for the photo shoot and was able to visit the de la Ossa chapel, the old family homes, and the cemetery of which Ramón speaks. Ramón is currently attending barber college with his veterans' benefits and hopes to attain his license by the spring of 2004. He will work as a barber until he is eligible to receive retirement benefits. Amy is doing foster care full-time until they can get back on their feet financially and are able to return to their beloved ranch in the San Rafael Valley.

About the Author

Patricia Preciado Martin is a native Arizonan and a magna cum laude graduate of the University of Arizona. She is the author of two other collections of oral history also published by the University of Arizona Press: *Images and Conversations: Mexican Americans Recall a Southwestern Past* (winner of the Virginia McCormick Scully Award for the best history by a Chicano/a or Native American) and *Songs My Mother Sang to Me: An Oral History of Mexican American Women.* The University of Arizona Press has also published three collections of her widely anthologized short stories: *Days of Plenty, Days of Want; El Milagro and Other Stories;* and *Amor Eterno: Eleven Lessons of Love. Amor Eterno* was the recipient of the Border Regional Library Association Southwest Book Award for fiction the year of its publication. Martin is active on the speakers' circuit both regionally and nationally and has received the Arizona Humanities Council Distinguished Public Scholar Award of Excellence. She met Jim, her husband of forty years, while serving in the Peace Corps in Central America. They live in Tucson.

About the Photographer

For more than thirty-five years native Arizonan José Galvez has used black-and-white photography to document Mexican American culture. He majored in journalism at the University of Arizona and upon graduation became a staff photographer for the *Arizona Daily Star.* In 1984, while at the *Los Angeles Times,* he led a photography staff that along with a team of reporters won a Pulitzer Prize in Community Service for a series on the Latino experience in southern California. Galvez's photographs have been exhibited in countless museums and galleries, including the Smithsonian. His first book, *Vatos,* was published in 2000. Today, he continues to document Mexican American communities across the United States, portraying his heritage in a realistic and positive fashion.